TAROT MAGIC

SPELLS, SPREADS, AND SORCERY USING THE TAROT DECK

I0458393

GREGORY LEE WHITE

White Willow Press
Nashville, TN

Tarot Magic
Spells, Spreads, and Sorcery Using the Tarot Deck
by
Gregory Lee White

Copyright © 2025 Gregory Lee White
gregoryleewhite.com

No part of this publication may be reproduced, distributed, or transmitted in
any form or by any means, including photocopying, recording, or other
electronic or mechanical methods, without the prior written permission of the
publisher. All rights reserved.

Text:
Gregory Lee White

Cover Art:
Gregory Lee White

Interior Illustrations:
various artists and illustrators from 1900 to the 2020s

First Edition 202

Published by
White Willow Press
211 Donelson Pike, Suite 111
Nashville, Tn 37214

Printed in the United States

ISBN: 978-1-965586-06-8

TABLE OF CONTENTS

OTHER BOOKS BY GREGORY LEE WHITE

Clucked – The Tale of Pickin Chicken

Making Soap from Scratch: How to Make Handmade Soap – A Beginners Guide and Beyond

Essential Oils and Aromatherapy - How to Use Essential Oils for Beauty, Health, and Spirituality

Little House Search – A Puzzle Book and Tour of the Works of Laura Ingalls Wilder

The Use of Magical Oils in Hoodoo, Prayer, and Spellwork

Papa Gee's Hoodoo Herbal - The Magic of Herbs, Roots, and Minerals in the Hoodoo Tradition

The Stranger in the Cup – How to Read Your Luck and Fate in the
Tea Leaves by Gregory Lee White and Catherine Yronwode

How to Use Amulets, Charms, and Talismans in the Hoodoo and Conjure Tradition
by Catherine Yronwode and Gregory Lee White

Lenormand Basics – How to Read Lenormand Cards for Beginners

Casting Love Spells – Rituals of Romance, Passion, and Attraction

Hex Appeal – How to Cast Dark Spells of Revenge, Cursing, and Damnation

Fairy Lore and Myths

Papa Gee's Book of Candle Magic

Cernunnos – The Lord of Wild Things

Hecate – The Goddess of Witchcraft

INTRODUCTION

You can learn a lot about a person by how they treat their tarot deck. Some keep theirs wrapped in silk, others tuck them under their pillow or place them in a box on the altar like a sacred relic. And then there are folks like me—who shuffle with one hand while stirring a pot with the other, cards laid out beside burning candles, a jar of honey, or a bowl of graveyard dirt. Because tarot isn't just for reading. It's for doing. It's a tool of magic as much as it is a mirror for the spirit.

Somewhere along the line, tarot got fenced in. People started acting like the cards belonged only on velvet-draped tables or in psychic fairs. I want to show you another side of tarot. The practical, gritty, spell-casting side.

This book is about working with the tarot as a magical ally. We'll talk about charging cards with intention, choosing the right layout for spellwork, and combining the cards with candles, oils, roots, and charms. We'll explore how to turn spreads into rituals and readings into results. Whether you're sweetening a lover, crossing an enemy, finding clarity, or calling in abundance—there's a card for that.

So if you're ready to work with the cards in a way that's bold, magical, and rooted in real tradition, then grab your favorite deck. We're about to wake the cards up and put them to work.

DEDICATION

To all the tarot and oracle readers I've had the joy of
reading beside through the years—at Pagan Pride Day
fundraisers, behind tables at psychic fairs, in the quiet
corners of metaphysical shops, and over coffee just for
the love of the cards.

Thank you for sharing the table, the stories, and the spirit
of the work. And to Fred and all the readers at
Hoodoo Psychics who not only read the cards but
mix in the most amazing magical advice.

A Brief History of Tarot

The tarot didn't begin as a magical tool. It wasn't birthed under a full moon or handed down from secret priesthoods in hushed whispers. In truth, its early days were far more ordinary—simple playing cards passed around noble courts and tavern tables. But like many powerful things, what started as a game eventually took root in deeper soil.

We know the first tarot-like cards showed up in Europe around the late 1300s. Back then, the decks were small, just four suits, and weren't meant for fortune-telling or ritual work. They were used for card games like *tarocchi* in Italy and *tarot* in France. If magic lingered in those early decks, it was sleeping quietly, waiting for the right time to wake up.

In the early 1400s, a transformation began. Artists started adding a fifth suit to some decks—illustrated cards that stood apart from the rest. These extra cards, rich with symbolic images of people, animals, and mysterious figures, were called "triumphs." Over time, they evolved into what we now know as the **Major Arcana**—the spiritual backbone of the modern tarot.

For a long while, tarot remained a game of the elite. The printing press hadn't yet spread its wings, so each card was painted by hand. Only those with wealth and status could afford a deck. But the imagery was already whispering secrets. Even in its early forms, the tarot was beginning to speak.

It wasn't until the 1700s that tarot stepped firmly into the realm of mysticism. A man named Antoine Court de Gébelin looked at the cards and declared they weren't just artwork—they were ancient, powerful, and packed with hidden wisdom. He claimed they came from Egypt, encoded with spiritual truths passed down through the ages. Whether that's historically accurate or not (spoiler: it's probably not), his words struck a chord. Suddenly, the tarot wasn't just a game. It was a key.

Around the same time, a French occultist by the name of Jean-Baptiste Alliette—better known as **Etteilla**—started publishing guides on how to read the cards for divination. He assigned meanings to each card, tied them to astrology and alchemy, and created one of the first structured systems for reading tarot as a magical act. His work helped shift the tarot out of the drawing room and into the ritual circle.

The real explosion came in the 1800s and 1900s, during the occult revival that swept through Europe. Secret societies like the Hermetic Order of the Golden Dawn incorporated tarot into their teachings and rituals. Tarot was now fully embedded in the world of Western esotericism. The archetypes became doorways. The suits became elements. The cards were no longer playthings—they were tools for transformation.

It was during this time that the most iconic deck was born: the **Rider-Waite-Smith Tarot**, created in 1909. Artist **Pamela Colman Smith** infused every card with layers of meaning, myth, and movement. This deck made it easier than ever to interpret the imagery intuitively, and it quickly became the standard for modern readers. To this day, it's still the deck I reach for most often—though there are now hundreds of beautiful variations, from gothic to glitter-covered, and everything in between.

By the time we reached the 20th and 21st centuries, tarot had evolved again. Decks began popping up that reflected not just old myths and ancient gods, but pop culture, feminism, decolonial spirituality, shadow work, queer identity, and every spiritual path under the sun. What was once a tightly held mystery became a tool for everyone. Today, tarot readers come from all walks of life—some cast spells with it, others journal with it, and some just want to know if their ex is coming back.

Even now, in some parts of Europe, tarot is still used strictly for gameplay. But for the rest of us—witches, rootworkers, spiritual seekers, and curious souls—it's much more than that. Tarot is a mirror. A guide. A storyteller. A spirit-touched language that speaks in symbols, signs, and intuition.

So the next time you hold a deck in your hands, pause for a moment. What you're holding isn't just 78 cards. It's a centuries-old conversation between human beings and the mysteries of the universe. It's a tool that has survived wars, revolutions, religious persecution, and the rise and fall of empires. It's been shuffled by gamblers and mystics alike. And somehow, it found its way to you. That alone makes it sacred.

THE HIGH PRIESTESS

Quick Tip: Using the High Priestess to Find a Lost Object
Place the High Priestess card on your altar or reading table, face up. Light a white or silver candle beside it, and sit quietly with the card. Ask her to reveal what is hidden. Close your eyes and breathe slowly, allowing an image or location to rise in your mind's eye. The High Priestess rules intuition, secrets, and the unseen—trust the first place that comes to you, even if it doesn't make sense right away. She often speaks in symbols, so look for clues, not just direct answers.

TAROT AND MAGIC

There's something about a tarot card that pulls at the soul—a whisper in the ink, a weight in the symbols. To most people, it's a tool for divination. But for magical practitioners, tarot is more than a way to peek at the future—it's a working tool, a magical instrument, and a living spellbook.

For centuries, the tarot was used mainly to tell fortunes and gain insight. The mystical side of the cards began to bloom in the 1700s, when occultists started linking them to astrology, numerology, and the Kabbalistic Tree of Life. Some claimed the cards were remnants of ancient Egyptian wisdom, encoded with secrets lost to time. That part's a stretch—but what's not a stretch is how deeply these symbols can reach into the heart of a magical working.

Tarot's role in spellwork really started to take shape in the late 1800s and early 1900s, right when the Western occult world was waking back up. The cards weren't just being read anymore—they were being used. Used in rituals. Used to focus energy. Used to open portals between the intention and the outcome.

Each card in the tarot holds its own spirit, its own current of energy. Think of them like magical allies. When you bring a tarot card into your spellwork, you're not just choosing a symbol—you're inviting a force into your ritual space. You're asking that force to lend its power to your intention. And if you choose the right cards, you're not just sending a wish into the universe—you're shaping the outcome with focused will.

Let's say you're working a spell for abundance. You could call in **The Empress**, who carries the lush fullness of the earth, or the **Ace of Pentacles**, a seed of prosperity waiting to grow. If you're working to strengthen your will or focus, **The Magician** is your go-to—he's the master of tools and talent, turning raw potential into real results.

These cards aren't passive. They anchor energy. They act as mirrors, amplifiers, and messengers. When you lay one down in a ritual, you're creating a focal point. It tells the universe what you're calling in—and it tells your spirit how to stay aligned.

Tarot can also be used for protection, cleansing, and banishing. Cards like **The Tower** or **The Devil** might not be cozy, but they're fierce when it comes to clearing out what no longer serves you. Need to shatter a harmful pattern or break someone's grip on your energy? The Tower has no problem burning things to the ground so you can start again.

The magic isn't just in the card—it's in how you work with it. Some practitioners place the cards on their altars. Others sleep with them under their pillow. Some bury them in the earth as part of a spell, or burn them (photocopies, not your actual deck!) to release their energy into the wind. Some pair them with herbs, oils, or crystals that share the same energy to build a spell that's layered and personal.

And then there's the matter of intuition. Tarot won't work for you if you're only going by a book. You have to feel the card. Let it speak. The way **The Lovers** shows up in your spell may be different than how it shows up for someone else—and that's not only okay, that's the point. Magic isn't one-size-fits-all, and neither is tarot.

So what makes tarot so powerful in spellcasting? It's simple: the cards hold story, symbol, and archetype. They contain every human experience—grief, joy, power, loss, transformation, rebirth. That means you can find a card that speaks to whatever energy you're trying to work with. And when you work with that card intentionally, you're not just casting a spell— you're casting a story, and you're deciding how it ends.

The trick is knowing which cards to call, and when. It's about timing, energy, and focus. It's about letting the cards carry your intention like a banner in the wind. Some cards spark action. Some guide healing. Some protect. Some destroy. Some build. You just have to choose the right tool for the job—and tarot gives you 78 to work with.

CHOOSING THE TAROT DECK THAT IS RIGHT FOR YOU

Let the Art Speak First
Tarot is a visual language. If a deck's imagery stirs something in your chest—curiosity, excitement, even a little fear—it's probably trying to talk to you. Trust the pull. Your spirit knows what it needs before your mind catches up.

Hold It, If You Can
If you're in a shop, pick the deck up. Feel its weight. Notice how your body reacts. Some decks feel warm and alive, while others sit cold in the hand. Your physical reaction can tell you more than any online review ever could.

Study the System Behind the Style
Most decks follow the Rider-Waite-Smith structure, but some veer into Thoth or Marseille traditions. If you're new, start with something that offers clear imagery and a companion guide. Complexity can come later—clarity is magic, too.

Ask What Kind of Magic You'll Be Doing
Different decks serve different purposes. Want a deck for shadow work? Look for one with darker, introspective art. Need something for spellcasting? Go with a deck whose symbols feel active and spell-ready. Divination? An honest, straightforward deck with expressive faces and clear suits is ideal.

It's Okay to Own More Than One
You don't have to marry your first deck. Like candles or herbs, different decks carry different energies. One might be for love spells, another for spirit work, and another just for reading others. Let them serve the purpose they were made for.

TAPPING INTO THE POWER

Tarot isn't just a deck of cards—it's a tool, a map, and a magical companion. The power in these 78 cards doesn't come from some outside force. It comes from the way they connect to your spirit, your intention, and the hidden rhythms of the world around you. Whether you're casting spells or seeking guidance, the tarot can do more than "tell the future." It can help you shape it.

Let's break down the most common ways to work with tarot—not just for reading, but for real magic.

DIVINATION

This is the most familiar use of tarot, and probably how most folks find their way in. Divination is the art of asking questions and receiving answers. When you shuffle the deck and lay down the cards, you're opening a door to your intuition—and to the spirit world, if that's your path.

But here's the thing: tarot isn't fortune-telling in the way people think. It doesn't tell you exactly what's going to happen. What it *does* show you is what's likely to unfold based on the path you're currently walking. It shines a light on what's hidden, what's influencing your situation, and what might need to shift.

I always tell people—think of a tarot reading like a snapshot of this moment in time. It's a reflection of what's going on beneath the surface and a glimpse into what *could* happen if you stay on your current course. But nothing is set in stone. Free will is always part of the picture.

Let's say you pull the **Death** card. That doesn't mean someone's going to die. It usually points to a transformation, a necessary ending. It's telling you something is falling away—something that needs to go so you can grow. If you resist it, the energy gets harder. But if you work with it, you can move through the change with power.

The more you practice reading, the more you'll see how flexible the cards are. Their meanings shift depending on the question, the person, and the energy in the room. That's why no two readings are ever the same.

SPELLWORK

Tarot shines in spellcasting. When you pull a card and place it in a working, it becomes a living symbol of your intent.

Say you're doing a love spell. You might use **The Lovers** card, or **Two of Cups**, to represent connection and harmony. If it's a prosperity spell, you could call on **The Ten of Pentacles** for long-term wealth and family success, or **The Ace of Pentacles** for new opportunities and fresh financial energy.

The suits also matter. Pentacles are tied to earth and money. Cups speak to love and emotions. Wands spark action and creativity. Swords cut through confusion and bring truth. You can build entire rituals using cards that match the energy you're working with.

It's not just about the image. The colors, the elements, even the numbers on the cards all carry energy. If you're doing a spell with **The Empress**, you might include roses or herbs for fertility. If you're working with **The Star**, maybe you bring in a glass of spring water or burn a candle dressed with glittering herbs. Let the card guide you—and then build your spell around it.

MEDITATION AND VISUALIZATION

Tarot cards make excellent companions for meditation. Pick a card that holds the energy you want to embody. Maybe you're working on confidence, so you sit with **The Sun**. Or you need healing and hope, so you focus on **The Star**.

Hold the card, look into it. Study the colors, the movement, the faces. Let your mind wander into the scene. If the card shows a garden, imagine stepping into it. If it shows a river, hear the water rushing past. Let the card's energy sink into your spirit.

This isn't about memorizing meanings. It's about connection. When you meditate with a tarot card, you build a relationship with it—and over time, those relationships become powerful tools in your magical practice.

Visualization is similar, but more active. Instead of observing, you become the energy of the card. Trying to manifest success? See yourself as **The Magician**—hands outstretched, all the tools before you, ready to call your desire into form. Let that image burn into your mind until it feels real.

PATHWORKING

Pathworking is a deeper kind of guided journey—part meditation, part spirit-travel. It's often done with the **Major Arcana**, since each card represents a stage of the soul's evolution.

To begin, choose a card that matches something you're working through. Sit with it until the imagery becomes vivid. Then, in your mind, step into the card. Walk into the landscape. Talk to the figures. Ask questions. Observe everything.

If you're working with **The Hermit**, you might find yourself standing at the edge of a cliff with a lantern in your hand, looking down into the valley below. Maybe you meet a guide. Maybe you discover something buried deep inside yourself. Whatever happens, the experience becomes part of your magical development.

This kind of journey can be intense. Keep a journal nearby. Write down what you saw, what you felt, and what messages came through. Over time, these journeys add layers of wisdom to your tarot practice—and to your spirit.

ENERGY WORK

You can also use tarot cards in chakra healing, aura cleansing, and general energy work. Each card has its own frequency. Some vibrate with grounding energy. Others clear the mind or open the heart.

Let's say you're feeling anxious and scattered. You might place **The Emperor** card at your feet during meditation to help bring structure and stability to your aura. If you're feeling stuck in grief, **The Moon** might help bring those hidden feelings to the surface where they can be healed.

Some people place tarot cards directly on the body during energy work—laying **The Star** over the heart, or **Strength** over the solar plexus. Others use them in grid layouts with crystals and herbs. Trust your instincts. If it feels right, it probably is.

RITUALS

Tarot cards can act as offerings, altar pieces, or stand-ins for gods and spirits. Let's say you're working with Aphrodite—**The Empress** makes a perfect representation of her energy. Set the card on your altar with roses, shells, or honey, and speak your intentions aloud.

You can also build entire rituals around the cards. For example, a three-card spread could represent where you are, what needs to be released, and what you're calling in. Or lay out a circle of cards to form a sacred boundary around your working.

The beauty of tarot is its flexibility. You can use it to amplify your magic, ground your focus, or add new depth to rituals you already know and love.

PUTTING IT ALL TOGETHER

You don't need to memorize a hundred definitions or recite meanings like flashcards. What you need is connection. Learn your deck. Feel the energy of each card. Let them become part of your magical language. Because the real magic isn't in the cardstock—it's in the way the symbols speak to your spirit.

Whether you're pulling one card for clarity or building a full ritual with herbs and fire and chant, remember this: tarot responds to intention. The more heart you put into it, the more it gives back.

And that's the real power of tarot—not just knowing what the cards mean, but knowing how to let them *work with you.*

UNDERSTANDING THE TAROT DECK

Before you can work real magic with your tarot deck, you need to understand what you're holding. This isn't just a stack of pretty cards. It's a complete system—a magical language made up of symbols, elements, numbers, and archetypes. Every card speaks, and every part of the deck carries a specific kind of energy. When you learn to hear those voices, the deck becomes more than a tool. It becomes an extension of your intuition.

The tarot is made up of 78 cards. These are divided into two main sections: the Major Arcana and the Minor Arcana. Think of the Major Arcana as the big-picture chapters of your life—the soul lessons, turning points, and initiations. The Minor Arcana, on the other hand, is where the day-to-day energy lives. It shows you the small details, the practical steps, and the shifts happening beneath the surface.

The Major Arcana consists of 22 cards, beginning with The Fool (0) and ending with The World (21). These cards represent deep, spiritual forces—birth, growth, transformation, and completion. They don't just describe events; they reflect the journey of the soul. Each one is a powerful archetype. When you draw a Major Arcana card, it means something big is stirring. A lesson, a challenge, or a gift is making itself known.

The Fool's Journey is the name often given to the storyline these cards follow. The Fool begins the journey naive and open-hearted, and along the way, he encounters teachers, trials, allies, and revelations. From The Magician who teaches focus, to The Tower that shakes your foundation, to The World where integration is complete—the Major Arcana traces the sacred map of spiritual awakening.

The Minor Arcana contains 56 cards, divided into four suits: Cups, Wands, Swords, and Pentacles. Each suit corresponds to an element:

- Cups: Water (emotions, intuition, relationships)
- Wands: Fire (action, passion, willpower)
- Swords: Air (thoughts, truth, communication)
- Pentacles: Earth (money, health, home, work)

Each suit has ten numbered cards and four Court Cards (Page, Knight, Queen, King). The numbered cards show progress—from beginnings (Ace) to completions (Ten). The Court Cards, on the other hand, are more personal. They represent people, personalities, or aspects of yourself or others. They also show how energy behaves at different levels of experience and expression.

The Court Cards in tarot are often the most misunderstood, but they carry powerful energy in both readings and magical work. They can represent real people, aspects of yourself, or even spiritual allies depending on the question and the context. Some folks see them as personality types. Others see them as stages of development. Either way, they give form and face to the energy of each suit.

The court is made up of four ranks: Pages, Knights, Queens, and Kings—each one aligned with its suit's element.

Kings are the masters of their domain. They represent authority, wisdom, and long-term experience. Kings are not always men, but they often speak to masculine energy—external, directive, and goal-oriented. When a King shows up in a reading or spell, you're dealing with someone who knows what they want and how to get it. Or, it may be a call for you to step into leadership and claim your throne.

- King of Wands: The fire of fire. This is someone who leads with vision and passion. A risk-taker, a trailblazer, someone who sparks ideas and lights up rooms. He may be an entrepreneur, artist, or spiritual leader—anyone bold enough to create something from nothing.
- King of Cups: Water made wise. Emotionally mature, diplomatic, and compassionate. He knows how to hold space for others without drowning in their feelings. He's calm in chaos, a steady hand during storms. This card may represent a healer, counselor, or anyone who leads from the heart.
- King of Swords: Air in its clearest, sharpest form. This is logic, truth, and intellectual power. He seeks justice, speaks with precision, and doesn't suffer fools. He could be a judge, a strategist, or a truth-teller whose words cut through the fog.

- King of Pentacles: The solid rock. Earth energy at its peak. He brings wealth, stability, and long-term vision. Think of a successful business owner or a provider who builds legacies and protects what he loves through planning and grounded action.

Queens represent internal mastery. They carry the feminine expression of their element—nurturing, wise, and deeply intuitive. Queens know how to hold power without needing to dominate. They reflect the heart and soul of their suit. When a Queen appears, look for emotional intelligence, quiet strength, and embodied wisdom.

- Queen of Wands: Fire with charisma. Confident, radiant, passionate. She lights up a room just by walking in. She's driven by purpose and isn't afraid to take the lead—but she leads with heart. Think of a performer, a teacher, or a spiritual leader who empowers others.
- Queen of Cups: Deep water. Empathetic, artistic, and emotionally attuned. She understands the undercurrents of emotion and helps others navigate theirs too. This could be a psychic, a therapist, or anyone who operates with gentle power and intuitive grace.
- Queen of Swords: Clear and cutting. She sees through lies and speaks uncomfortable truths when needed. She's honest, intelligent, and unapologetically sharp. She may be someone who's been through pain and turned it into wisdom. This card may represent a thinker,

writer, or leader who values clarity above all else.

- Queen of Pentacles: The ultimate earth mother. Practical, abundant, and grounded. She brings comfort, knows how to manage a home or business, and cares deeply for those around her. This is the healer, the herbalist, the provider who creates security through resourcefulness.

Knights are movers. They bring action and momentum, often with a little fire behind them— even the watery or earthy ones. Knights are rarely still. They carry the energy forward, acting as messengers or change agents. They often show up when a shift is underway or when something needs to get moving.

- Knight of Wands: Fiery and fast. This is the adventurer, the one who acts before he thinks. He brings bold ideas, big gestures, and lots of energy. Sometimes too much. In spellwork, he can help ignite passion or kick down doors, but he can also burn out quickly if not directed well.
- Knight of Cups: The romantic dreamer. He's water in motion—artistic, emotional, and poetic. He moves with his heart, not his head. This may represent a love interest, an invitation, or a call to follow your intuition. In magic, he brings charm, seduction, and emotional depth.
- Knight of Swords: Charging in with clarity. He acts fast, speaks with conviction, and often moves before he gets all the details. He's sharp, ambitious, and focused. This card

can help cut through confusion or push through obstacles, but be mindful of haste and tunnel vision.

- Knight of Pentacles: The slow and steady one. He's raw earth in motion—methodical, disciplined, and hardworking. He may not be flashy, but he gets the job done. In readings and spells, he brings patience, commitment, and long-term strategy.

Pages are the children of the tarot. They represent newness, potential, curiosity, and learning. Sometimes they show up as messages or as beginnings of something new—an idea, a relationship, a spiritual path. Other times, they reflect where you are still growing, still exploring.

- Page of Wands: Fire on the brink of ignition. Eager, enthusiastic, and bursting with potential. This Page is excited about what lies ahead and is ready to take the first step into adventure. Great for spells of new projects or rediscovering passion.
- Page of Cups: The sensitive dreamer. Open-hearted, imaginative, and emotionally raw. This card might show up when your intuition is awakening or when emotional healing is just beginning. Useful in rituals for self-love, art, and creative birth.
- Page of Swords: Always watching, always questioning. Curious, quick-minded, and full of ideas. He asks questions others might avoid and seeks knowledge wherever he can find it. Useful in spells that require clarity, new insight, or mental breakthroughs.

- Page of Pentacles: Earthy and earnest. Ambitious, practical, and learning to build. This Page may be starting a new job, a new path of study, or planting the seeds for long-term goals. A strong ally for money spells or anything involving growth and learning.

In magical work, Court Cards can also serve as proxies or poppets. You can use them to represent people involved in a situation or parts of yourself you're working with. If you're doing a working for love and pull the Knight of Cups, you might let him stand in for your future partner—or for the romantic part of yourself that's ready to emerge. If you're doing a binding and the King of Swords appears reversed, that might be the oppressive boss or authority figure you're trying to cut ties with.

You can even use the Court Cards on your altar to call in their qualities. If you need patience, meditate with the Knight of Pentacles. If you're stepping into a leadership role, sit with the Queen of Wands and invite her fire to rise in you.

The Court Cards ask you to look deeper. Who is showing up? What are they teaching you? And how can you embody or release the energy they bring? Because whether they appear as allies, warnings, or reflections of your own spirit, these figures don't just sit on the page. They come to life when you work with them.

READING THE DECK LIKE A WITCH

Understanding the parts of the deck gives you more control when you step into spellwork. Want to call in abundance? Pull from the **Pentacles**. Need protection or energy to move forward? The **Wands** have your back. Working through emotional pain or relationship issues? **Cups** will show you where the heart needs tending. Trying to break through confusion or speak a hard truth? You'll find your clarity in the **Swords**.

You don't need to memorize every meaning. Just start paying attention. Notice how each card feels. Watch how they show up in your life, how they react when placed in spells, how they shift your energy when you meditate with them. The deck is your magical partner. It's not just about what each card means—it's about how they work with you.

Learn the structure so you can break it when needed. Know the rules so you can bend them in service of your craft. Once you understand how the deck is built, you can begin to shape it like a magical language. And that's when things really start to move.

TAROT SPREADS FOR SPELLCASTING

A tarot spread isn't just a way to lay down cards—it's a magical map. In spellwork, it becomes a layout of power, a blueprint to focus your energy and give shape to your desire. When you design a spread with intention, you're doing more than asking for answers. You're building a structure where spirit and spell can meet.

Most people think of spreads as tools for readings. But when used in magic, a tarot spread becomes a ritual all on its own. Every card position becomes a doorway. Every layout becomes a sacred shape. The spread becomes the bones of the spell, and the cards bring it to life.

You can use a traditional spread—like a three-card layout—or you can create your own from scratch. Making your own spreads is an act of magical authorship. It allows you to tailor the working to your intention, your spirit, and the kind of energy you want to call in. There are no strict rules here. Only rhythm, purpose, and intuition.

Start with your goal. What are you casting for? Clarity? Protection? Prosperity? Are you trying to mend a broken relationship, open the way forward, or remove something that's holding you back? Be clear. The more specific you are, the easier it is to build a spread that actually moves energy.

Once you know what you're working toward, begin shaping the layout. Maybe your spread will be a triangle to raise power and direct it upward. Maybe it forms a circle to contain energy and hold it safely in place. Or maybe you're walking a line from the past to the future and placing the cards along that thread. The way you lay the cards becomes part of the magic.

Give each position a purpose. For a love working, you might create spaces for the desire, the blockage, the needed shift, and the possible outcome. If you're casting for courage, the spread could include what you're afraid of, what strength lies hidden, what must be faced, and what power you already hold. You can use as few or as many cards as you like. What matters is that each one holds a job within the working.

Charging the spread is just as important as laying it out. This is where you feed the layout with energy. You can use candlelight, breathwork, herbs, crystals, or simply the focus of your will. Hold your intention clearly in mind and project it into the space where the cards will be placed. Call upon your spirits, ancestors, or deities if you work with them. Ask them to walk with you as you open the spread.

As you place each card, breathe with it. Let your energy sink into the space. See the card not as a prediction, but as a spell component—an anchor of energy that holds part of the whole. The image, the symbolism, even the number on the card—all of it becomes part of the ritual.

Once all cards are laid, read the spread aloud if it helps you solidify your work. Speak to the spirits, speak to yourself, speak to the spell. Naming what you see gives it life. If a card feels wrong or if the energy is off, trust your instincts. You can adjust the layout, move a card, or even swap one out if the message isn't landing right. This is your working. The cards are here to serve the spell—not the other way around.

Don't be afraid to repeat the spread on multiple days if needed. Some workings require more than one session to unfold. Others may shift as you begin to move energy and create change. Keep a record of what you've done. Write down the cards you used, the shape of the spread, and how the energy felt. This kind of magical journaling becomes a personal grimoire of successful workings and evolving wisdom.

Let's look at a few example spreads to spark your creativity.

A simple three-card manifestation spread might look like this: Card one is your current energy. Card two is your obstacle. Card three is the outcome you're calling in. This spread works well when paired with candle magic or intention setting, especially during the waxing moon.

For banishing work, you might use a five-card cross layout. The center card is the unwanted energy. The four cards around it represent what's feeding it, what it's doing to your life, what you must do to release it, and what will fill the space once it's gone.

A healing spread could be built in the shape of a heart. Each card placed inside the curve carries a layer of restoration—what needs healing, what's blocking the process, what support is available, and what strength lies within.

You can also create seasonal or moon-based spreads. Try a lunar wheel for spellwork tied to the moon cycle. New moon at the top, waxing and waning crescents to the sides, full moon at the base. Each position matches the energy of that moon phase and guides your spell through a natural rhythm.

One of my favorite power layouts is the triangle— three cards for the three faces of a working. The first card is the root of the situation. The second is the energy you're calling in. The third is the shift that will come when the spell takes hold. This spread is simple, strong, and easy to weave into almost any kind of ritual.

Remember, you don't need to be an expert to create a spread. You don't have to know every card by heart. All you need is intention, clarity, and the courage to follow your own voice. The more you work this way, the more natural it becomes. Over time, you'll develop your own library of spreads—layouts you return to again and again, each one shaped by your hand and powered by your magic.

A tarot spread isn't just for reading. It's for casting. For shaping energy. For telling the universe what you want and showing it exactly how to listen.

And once you learn to lay your cards with purpose, you're not just reading the future—you're writing it.

PRACTICAL MAGIC WITH TAROT

If tarot cards are the bones of your magical practice, then correspondences are the muscle and sinew that hold it all together. They connect everything—symbols, colors, herbs, numbers, planetary influences—and they're what help your spellwork move with precision and power. When you add correspondences to your tarot practice, you're layering the magic. You're speaking the universe's language in stereo.

Each card in the tarot already holds its own energy. But when you match that card with the right herb, stone, candle color, or planetary hour, you're amplifying its message. You're creating a whole atmosphere around the intention. That's where the magic deepens.

Take **The High Priestess** for example. She's mystery, intuition, hidden knowledge. On her own, she invites you into the space between the veils. But if you light a blue candle, burn some mugwort, and place a piece of moonstone next to the card while doing trancework or divination—you're not just reading cards anymore. You're stepping fully into her temple.

That's what magical correspondences do. They help you set the stage for each spell and reading. They let your tools, your space, and your spirit all move in harmony.

Start by choosing a card that reflects the energy you're working with. If you're casting for transformation, you might reach for **Death**, **The Tower**, or **Judgement**. If you're seeking love, maybe it's **The Lovers**, **Two of Cups**, or **The Empress**. Once you've chosen the card, pull together items that match its energy. You're looking to build a web—a magical ecosystem around that image.

For example, let's say you're working a spell with **The Magician**. This card is all about personal power, manifestation, and making something out of nothing. To support that energy, you could work at noon (the hour of the sun), dress a yellow candle with frankincense oil, place a citrine crystal on your altar, and burn a pinch of basil. Each of these items aligns with solar energy, mental clarity, and creative will— all things **The Magician** stands for. What you've done is take the concept of the card and anchored it into the physical world.

That's the real trick with practical tarot magic. You're turning symbols into spells.

You can also create custom combinations based on your own experiences. Maybe **The Chariot** always feels like Mars to you, even though some traditions tie it to Cancer. That's fine. Magic responds to personal connection more than textbook definitions. Use what works. If rosemary makes you feel strong and steady, then pair it with a card like **Strength** or **The Emperor** in your workings. Keep notes. Build your own personal grimoire of correspondences. Over time, it becomes a reference that no book can beat—because it's rooted in your magic.

Tarot can also act as a magical trigger when paired with elemental energy. The suits already correspond to the elements—Wands with Fire, Cups with Water, Swords with Air, and Pentacles with Earth. If you're doing spellwork with the **Ace of Wands**, bring fire into the mix. Light a red candle. Burn cinnamon or clove. Use heat to activate the intention. If you're using a **Cups** card, work with water—tea, rosewater, moon water, even a bowl of saltwater charged under the moon. Let the element carry the card's energy further.

You can use multiple cards in a working too. That's where the layering gets rich. Want to attract a new job? Combine **The Magician**, **Eight of Pentacles**, and **Ten of Pentacles**. That's initiation, work ethic, and long-term success all in one spread. Add a green candle, some patchouli, and a pyrite stone, and you've built a full spell using both image and matter.

Numbers also matter. All the cards carry a number, and that number carries meaning. Ones are beginnings. Twos are duality and decisions. Threes are growth. Fours bring stability. Fives stir chaos. Sixes ask for harmony. Sevens challenge you to have faith. Eights bring power and repetition. Nines move toward completion. Tens are the end of one cycle and the beginning of another. When you build a spell with multiple cards, pay attention to the numbers. Do they reinforce each other or conflict? That can tell you a lot about how the energy will behave once the spell is set in motion.

Color plays a huge role too. Look at the dominant colors in a card when choosing candle colors, altar cloths, or dressings. **The Sun** is full of gold and yellow—so use solar energy, gold foil, or sunflower petals to amplify it. **The Moon** is soaked in blue, silver, and black—so lean into night magic, reflective surfaces, and watery movement when working with that card.

And don't overlook the seasons or planetary hours. Pulling **The Hermit** during winter has a different feel than pulling him in summer. He may call you inward in the dark season, or ask you to retreat from the heat of outer pressure in the bright months. Context adds flavor.

You can also flip it: choose the spell you want to do, and then go looking for the cards that match. Doing a cleansing? Choose cards like **The Star**, **Temperance**, or **Ace of Cups**. Want to call in courage? Work with **Strength**, **The Sun**, or **The Chariot**. Layer them with your other spell ingredients and let the cards act as both sigils and energetic mirrors.

Don't be afraid to get creative. The tarot is a system, yes—but it's also an invitation. You're allowed to color outside the lines. If you want to tape cards under your altar to radiate their energy throughout your space, do it. If you want to carry a card in your pocket like a charm, go for it. If you want to bury one in the garden to help a dream grow, trust your instinct. The only real rule is to treat the deck with respect. It's a sacred tool, but it's not fragile. It wants to be used.

One last word on this: the cards are not the magic. *You* are. The cards are messengers, mirrors, keys. But the energy they stir comes from you. When you add correspondences, you're giving your spell more texture, more shape. You're weaving a stronger thread. But the thread still begins with your will.

Use the cards to open the door. Let the herbs, stones, and symbols speak alongside them. Build spells like poetry—intuitive, layered, powerful. The tarot will meet you where you are. And if you use it with intention, it will carry your magic farther than you ever imagined.

Quick Tip: For money magic, use the *Ten of Pentacles* or *Ace of Pentacles* as a focal point. Anoint the card with a drop of money-drawing oil and place it beneath a green candle dressed with cinnamon and basil. Let the card act as a magnet for prosperity while the flame carries your intention into the spirit world.

RITUALS AND TAROT

Rituals are where intention becomes reality. They're the places where breath, movement, and spirit come together to make magic. When you bring tarot into ritual, you're not just using cards as decoration or divination—you're using them as active participants. Every card becomes a spell in its own right, a vessel that can hold energy, embody a deity, or open a door between the seen and unseen.

Tarot is more than a tool—it's a living system of archetypes. Each card in the deck represents a current of energy that runs through the human experience. The Major Arcana especially holds ritual potency. These 22 cards are big medicine. They speak to spiritual lessons, life initiations, and the movements of the soul. When called into a ritual setting, they do more than mirror what's happening—they help shape it.

Say you're calling on **The Fool** in a rite to start a new journey. That card becomes a guide. It invites in openness, wonder, and a fearless leap of faith. If you're invoking **The Magician**, you're calling down the power of focused will—the ability to turn thought into form. **Death** brings release and transformation. **The Empress** opens the gates of abundance and creation. These aren't just ideas—they're energies that respond when you call them with purpose.

Designing a tarot-based ritual starts with choosing your archetype. Ask yourself: what energy do I want to work with? What lesson am I being drawn to? What shift do I need to create in my life?

Once you've chosen the card—or cards—build your ritual around that theme. Start with purification. Clear your space using smoke, sound, salt, or whatever method suits your tradition. Lay out your altar. Place the chosen tarot card in a central position, as if it's a guest of honor. Light a candle, choose herbs or stones that align with the card's energy, and write out a simple invocation to speak aloud.

For example, if you're working with **The Lovers**, you might light two red or pink candles and place them on either side of the card. You could write down your intention for union or harmony and tie it with a red thread. Speak to the card as if it were a spirit. Ask it to guide your heart, restore connection, or help you make a clear decision from a place of love.

You don't need anything fancy. Even a bowl of water, a card, and your full attention can create a powerful working. What matters is that you stay focused, that your actions reflect your intention, and that you treat the card like a magical ally—not just a symbol, but a spirit you're calling into the circle.

Tarot rituals can also be done in stages. Some practitioners do them over several days, pulling a new card each day to build a layered working. You could do a seven-day ritual where each card represents a different phase of healing or growth. The act of showing up every day with intention deepens your connection—not just to the deck, but to yourself.

Don't forget to ground and close the ritual. Once the working is complete, thank the energies you've called in. Blow out the candles. Clear the space. Wrap the card in cloth, or place it somewhere sacred to let its energy continue to radiate. If you've written an intention or created a charm during the ritual, keep it on your altar, carry it with you, or bury it at a crossroads—whatever feels right for the work.

Now let's talk about aligning these rituals with the natural cycles.

The **moon phases** are powerful allies in ritual timing. During the **new moon**, work with cards that represent beginnings—like **The Fool, Ace of Wands**, or **The Magician**. At the **full moon**, pull in cards of fullness, truth, and radiance—**The Sun, The World, The Star**. During the **waning moon**, lean into release with cards like **Death, The Hanged Man**, or **Ten of Swords**.

You can also work with the **Wheel of the Year**. Each sabbat carries its own themes and energies, and tarot can bring those to life.

- At **Yule**, draw on **The Hermit, The Star**, or **The Sun** to reflect the return of light.

- At **Imbolc**, work with **The High Priestess, The Empress**, or **Ace of Pentacles** to awaken creativity and spark new intentions.

- At **Ostara**, focus on balance and growth with cards like **Justice, The Lovers**, or **Two of Pentacles**.

- At **Beltane**, bring in passion and fertility through **The Emperor**, **The Lovers**, or **Knight of Wands**.

- At **Litha**, when the sun is strongest, invoke **The Sun**, **Strength**, or **The World** for joy, completion, and celebration.

- At **Lammas**, call on **The Empress**, **Ten of Pentacles**, or **Queen of Pentacles** to honor harvest and gratitude.

- At **Mabon**, look to **Justice**, **The Hanged Man**, or **The Moon** for reflection, letting go, and restoring balance.

- At **Samhain**, walk with **Death**, **The High Priestess**, or **Judgement** to commune with spirits and walk between worlds.

These seasonal and lunar rituals don't have to be complicated. Even one candle, one card, and your spoken word is enough to move energy when done with heart.

You can also design your own archetypal rituals from scratch. For release, you might work with **The Tower**, write down what needs to fall away, and burn the paper as an offering. For healing, meditate with **The Star**, then pour water into the earth while naming your sorrows. For clarity, sit with **The Hermit** in silence and journal what comes. The beauty of tarot is that it already holds the structure—the image, the story, the energy. All you have to do is give it a voice.

Ritual doesn't have to look like something from a movie. It doesn't need robes, tools, or long incantations. It just needs to be sincere. Tarot helps you focus that sincerity. It helps you frame your magic, speak your desire, and hold yourself accountable to what you're asking for.

When you use tarot in ritual, you're stepping into the card. You're not just pulling a symbol—you're becoming the energy. That's when the work becomes real. That's when magic happens.

If you've been treating your tarot deck like a book of answers, it's time to see it for what it truly is: a grimoire, a mirror, and a door. And every time you place a card on your altar, you're opening that door with purpose.

Quick Tip for Using The World Card in Tarot Magic:
Use *The World* card to seal a spell or ritual when your goal is
completion, fulfillment, or successful closure. After casting your
intention—whether for love, career, or healing—place *The World*
card on your altar as a final energetic stamp. It locks in your work
and signals to the universe: *the cycle is complete, the goal is achieved,
and the energy is whole.*

MIXING TAROT AND FOLK MAGIC

Folk magic lives in the bones. It's handed down through stories, whispered advice, everyday objects that carry more power than they let on. It shows up in broom bristles behind doors, salt across thresholds, jars hidden behind stoves. It doesn't always come with ceremony—but it always comes with power.

Tarot, on the other hand, speaks in symbols. It tells stories that stretch across centuries, drawn in ink and layered with archetype. And while it might seem at first like folk magic and tarot live in different worlds, they actually work beautifully together. One is the voice of the people. The other, a mirror for the soul. When combined, they create a bridge between the seen and unseen, the practical and the spiritual, the inherited and the intuitive.

Let's start with protection, because folk magic is full of it—and tarot can lend its hand here in a big way. In folk traditions, people have always used charms, objects, and signs to guard the home and body. Tarot cards can become part of that protective web. Cards like **Strength**, **The Star**, or even **The Tower** hold their own kinds of power when placed with purpose.

Take **Strength**. In a protective charm, this card represents inner resilience—the kind that keeps you steady when others try to shake your foundation. You might place the Strength card inside a mojo bag, alongside high john root, iron filings, and a pinch of red pepper, then tuck it behind your front door. That card becomes a spiritual ally, keeping watch and offering spiritual backbone.

The Star works beautifully as a home blessing. Set her on your altar beside a bowl of water and a white candle. Speak a prayer for peace, harmony, and restful sleep. She's not just a symbol of hope—she becomes a beacon, drawing in clean, uplifting energy. On the other hand, **The Tower**, often feared in readings, can be your best friend in banishing work. In folk magic, sometimes you don't cleanse softly. Sometimes you break the thing that's harming you and scatter the pieces. The Tower holds that energy. Place it upside-down over the name of someone stirring up trouble, burn a black candle beside it, and let that storm pass through.

Folk magic is also about the home. Hearth. Family. Roots. It's about making your space sacred, even if all you have is a single shelf or a worn-out window ledge. Tarot fits right in. Use cards like the **Four of Wands**, **Ten of Pentacles**, or **Queen of Pentacles** as part of home blessing rituals. You might place one in the kitchen to keep your meals infused with love. Or on a family photo to bring stability and peace. Use **Three of Cups** to bring joy into the home—especially when you're preparing for guests or a gathering. Let those cards sit in a place of honor while you cook, sweep, and prepare. They become not just part of your spell—they become part of your space.

You can also read the energy of your home using tarot. Do a spread with this in mind. Lay one card at the threshold for what's entering, one in the center for what lives in the heart of the home, one in a dark corner or closet for what's hidden and forgotten. Let the cards show you what needs cleansing, what's thriving, and where energy might be stuck. This kind of folk-style house reading is simple but revealing. Once you see where the trouble is, you can go in and fix it—with salt, floor wash, prayers, and maybe another card to hold the blessing in place.

Now let's speak to the ancestors. Because no real folk magic leaves them out. Working with the dead is sacred, whether they're blood kin, chosen family, or spiritual lineage. Tarot can act as a bridge here too. It becomes a voice for those who've passed—one they can speak through, or one that helps us hear.

Some practitioners pull cards specifically to speak to their ancestors. You can set up an ancestor altar with offerings of food, drink, or tobacco. Light a candle and pull a card asking, "What message do you have for me?" or "How can I honor you today?" Cards like **The High Priestess**, **The Moon**, or **Judgement** often show up in this kind of work—they speak to hidden truths, spirit voices, and resurrection. If you pull **The Hermit**, perhaps they want solitude. If **The Lovers** appears, maybe they want reconciliation between family lines. If **Death** comes forward, it may be time to let go of something that no longer serves your bloodline.

You can also use tarot cards to build ancestor altars. Let them represent different family members or energies. Maybe **The Emperor** is your grandfather, **The Queen of Cups** your great-aunt who always knew things before they happened. Maybe you place **The World** in the center to represent the collective wisdom of all who came before. These cards can be dressed with oil, placed beneath photos, or tucked into folded notes containing prayers.

Tarot speaks when you let it, and the dead will often use whatever voice we offer them. Use the deck with respect when reaching across the veil. Keep a journal nearby to record anything that comes through, especially in dreams or sudden thoughts. These messages may come gently, but they carry weight.

Tarot also shines in folk spells that deal with attraction, binding, uncrossing, and setting things right. In these cases, the cards act like paper poppets. You can use them in place of photos when you don't have one—or layer them behind a target's name or petition paper.

For a spell to bring healing to someone, you might use **The Star** or **Three of Cups**. Write their name on a slip of paper, place the card over it, and bind them together with green thread soaked in healing oil. Keep it in a sacred space until the spell has run its course.

For banishing or crossing, cards like **Ten of Swords**, **The Tower**, or **The Devil** can be charged with that darker current. Sandwich a photo or name paper between two cards—perhaps **The Devil** and **Five of Swords**—then wrap it tightly with black string and tuck it away in a box of thorns. Again, use with caution and ethical clarity. Folk magic doesn't shy away from the sharp end of the blade, but it always respects the balance of cause and effect.

This method also works for reconciliation. Say you're trying to mend a bond or call someone home. Use

Two of Cups, **The Lovers**, or **Page of Cups**. Write your intention on parchment or brown paper, fold it toward you, and press it between the cards. Add rose petals or sugar if the sweetness is needed. Set it on your altar and speak their name over it each night.

This is tarot-as-talisman. Tarot-as-stand-in. Tarot as the physical representation of a person, place, emotion, or condition. Each card becomes a vessel. A mirror. A carrier of magic.

You can even create jar spells or charm bags around the energy of a card. Want abundance? Use **Ace of Pentacles**, add five coins, some cinnamon, basil, and a magnet. Seal it with green wax. Want clarity? Try **Ace of Swords**, rosemary, lemongrass, and a clear quartz point. Want to attract a specific kind of lover? Use **Knight of Cups** or **The Lovers**, with sugar, damiana, and a drop of your favorite perfume.

Tarot is flexible. It's willing. The cards don't demand ceremony, though they can hold it. What they do demand is intention. When brought into folk magic, tarot doesn't need to be reinterpreted or watered down—it just needs to be claimed. Let it speak in your spells. Let it carry your prayers. Let it stand on your altar like any candle, charm, or saint's image.

Because the truth is, tarot belongs in the kitchen just as much as the coven. It belongs in your pocket next to a red flannel bag. It belongs under the bed, above the door, or sealed in a jar buried in the yard. It's not too fancy for folk work—it's waiting to be included.

And when you bring the cards into your rootwork, your home blessings, and your ancestral veneration, you're not just blending systems.

You're honoring where magic has always lived—between the hands, at the hearth, and in the heart.

ELEMENTAL MAGIC

Tarot is built on elemental foundations. The suits are more than categories—they're living expressions of the primal forces that make up the universe. Earth, Air, Fire, and Water aren't just symbolic; they are spirits in their own right. And once you begin to see the elements as allies—rather than abstract ideas—you unlock a deeper level of power in your magic.

Each suit in the Minor Arcana is tied to an element, and through that connection, each card holds its own current of energy. The suits don't just describe your day-to-day experiences. They show you which elemental forces are moving through your life—and how to work with them, redirect them, or anchor them.

The suits align like this:

- **Wands** correspond with **Fire**

- **Cups** correspond with **Water**

- **Swords** correspond with **Air**

- **Pentacles** correspond with **Earth**

These aren't just poetic associations. They speak to real movement in your spirit and the environment around you. When you work with the tarot through an elemental lens, you're not just reading cards—you're conjuring with the same forces that shape storms, stones, flames, and tides.

Let's walk through each element and the suit it commands.

Fire – The Force of Creation and Destruction

The suit of **Wands** carries the blazing energy of fire. It's willpower. Action. Passion. Drive. But it also holds the capacity for burn-out, aggression, and restlessness. Fire builds. Fire destroys. Fire transforms.

Cards from the Wands suit show up when something needs to be done, created, or released. They're about motion. They ask, "What are you doing with your energy? Where are you putting your focus? What's lighting you up—or burning you down?" The Wands ignite creative energy and stir up the energy in the sacral chakra where creativity and sexuality is processed.

When working with fire energy in tarot, use candles, heat, smoke, and movement. Cast spells that call in confidence, ignite creativity, or blaze through resistance. Let **Ace of Wands** be your matchstrike. Let **Knight of Wands** be your fuel. But be mindful— fire doesn't ask permission, and it will consume more than you meant to offer if you're not grounded.

Rituals that tap into fire should feel alive. You might read your cards beside a fire pit, burn petitions under a new moon, or speak your intentions aloud with flame in your voice. Fire responds to boldness. Give it something real to burn.

Water – Emotion, Intuition, and Depth

Cups belong to water. This is the element of emotion, dreams, connection, and the subconscious. It flows, it heals, it drowns, and it reveals.

Water cards show you the state of your emotional and intuitive life. Are you open or guarded? Overflowing or empty? Do you need to release, or do you need to receive?

Working with water through the Cups means diving into feelings and letting intuition take the lead. These cards are perfect for spells involving love, healing, dreamwork, or ancestor communication. Think **Two of Cups** for harmony. **The Queen of Cups** for psychic depth. **The Moon** when things are shifting and unclear but powerful underneath.

In water rituals, use bowls, sacred wells, rivers, or moon water. Soak your tarot cards in light, not moisture. Bathe with intention. Speak to the water before you sip. Use tea and tincture as part of the working. Water responds to softness, rhythm, and truth. It doesn't care if you have the words—it only asks you to feel.

Air – Intellect, Clarity, and Motion

Swords are ruled by air. This is the element of the mind—ideas, truth, communication, and mental sharpness. Air moves fast. It cuts through illusion. But it can also stir up anxiety, conflict, and indecision.

Swords show up when thought is needed, or when overthinking has become the enemy. They challenge you to see clearly, speak honestly, and stop avoiding the hard conversations.

Work with air energy when you need clarity, focus, or justice. Call on **Ace of Swords** to cut away confusion. Use **King of Swords** when you need precision, strategy, or lawful insight. **Ten of Swords** may show a hard truth—but one that finally sets you free.

Air magic loves breath, words, and sound. Use incense, feathers, wind chimes, spoken incantations, or simply your voice in prayer. Cast spells on the wind, or whisper into the breeze. Write your thoughts down and burn the paper, letting the smoke carry your intent.

Air doesn't need ceremony. It needs honesty. The question is never just "what do you think?"—it's "what truth are you avoiding, and what will you say once you face it?"

Earth – Grounding, Growth, and Structure

Pentacles belong to earth. This is the realm of money, home, health, work, and physical well-being. Earth is slow, steady, fertile, and wise. It builds over time. It teaches patience. It holds the memory of every step you've ever taken.

Earth cards show where you're building—and where the foundation might need reinforcing. Are you stable? Are you supported? Are you investing in what will last?

Work with earth energy for prosperity spells, long-term health, or anything involving protection and rootedness. **Ace of Pentacles** brings new opportunities. **Nine of Pentacles** is abundance earned through work. **The King of Pentacles** governs legacy and mastery in the material world.

To connect with this energy, go outside. Touch soil. Tend plants. Use crystals, bones, wood, and salt. Create jar spells. Bury cards beneath your altar or plant them in ritual gardens.

Bringing the Elements Together

Once you understand how the elements live in the tarot, you can use that wisdom to build better spreads, stronger spells, and deeper rituals. Want balance? Try pulling one card from each suit to see which elemental energy is strongest or missing. Want to strengthen a spell? Make sure your correspondences line up—not just with the card you've chosen, but with the element it belongs to.

You can use elemental spreads to create harmony. Four cards, laid in a square:

- North: Earth (material support)

- East: Air (mental state)

- South: Fire (action and drive)

- West: Water (emotions and relationships)

Place a fifth card in the center to represent your spirit—the force tying them all together. That one could be a Major Arcana, or one you pull intuitively.

Tarot speaks in layers. The suits are just the beginning. The elements that power those suits bring movement, voice, and spirit to your magic. They remind us that nothing is ever truly still. Everything flows. Everything shifts. And with the tarot in your hands, you become part of that dance.

So the next time you draw a card, don't just look at the image—ask which element is speaking. What does it want from you? What can you offer in return?

Because once you start listening, the fire will answer. The water will move. The air will carry. And the earth will hold.

SHADOW WORK IN TAROT

There's a reason many people shuffle past the darker cards in the deck with a nervous glance or a forced smile. It's not just fear of what they'll find—it's fear of having to face what they already know. But here's the thing: if you want to work magic that actually changes things—if you want to cast spells that *heal*, that *break chains*, that *reclaim your power*—then you have to get comfortable walking in the dark. That's where shadow work begins. And tarot, when used intentionally, is one of the most honest, unflinching tools we have for doing it.

Shadow work isn't about fixing yourself. It's not about pretending you're broken so you can be more palatable to the world. It's about seeing what's been buried, repressed, or shamed—and choosing to meet it without fear. It's about taking back the parts of yourself that got shut away because they were too angry, too sensitive, too loud, too witchy, too anything. The shadow isn't evil. It's just the part of you that was cast aside. And in magic, anything that's been cast aside holds *tremendous power*—if you're brave enough to reclaim it. Tarot lays all of that bare.

When you sit down with your deck and say, "Show me what I'm not seeing," the cards don't hesitate. They show you your patterns. They show you where you sabotage yourself. They show you where your pain has turned into armor and where your fear has learned to speak in your voice. They also show you how to shift it—how to work with those energies, not against them. That's what makes tarot the perfect shadow work companion. It doesn't judge. It just reflects.

But reflection takes guts. The first step is being willing to pull the cards even when you don't want to see what they'll say. If you only ever pull when you're looking for a yes or hoping for reassurance, you're missing half the magic. Shadow work begins when you pull a card and your gut drops—and you stay. You don't shuffle it back into the deck or try to "reinterpret" it until it feels softer. You sit with it. You ask it why it showed up. You let it tell you the truth.

There are certain cards that tend to show up in shadow work again and again. Not because they're negative, but because they reflect the darker layers of the human experience.

The Tower. Death. The Devil. Five of Pentacles. Ten of Swords. The Moon. Even **The High Priestess** can be a shadow card when she's pointing you toward those secrets you're afraid to name.

These cards carry weight, and rightfully so. But they also carry potential. The Tower doesn't just tear things down—it clears the rubble so something stronger can be built. Death isn't just about endings— it's about release, about compost, about what feeds the roots of your future. The Devil doesn't just trap you—it teaches you where you've given your power away, and how to take it back.

In a shadow reading, these are the cards you don't shy away from. These are the ones you *invite in*. Light a black candle. Pull a spread that asks the hard questions. Let the deck dig in.

Here are a few spread ideas for shadow work using tarot. These can be done as one-time rituals or part of a longer self-healing journey.

The Root of the Wound
1. What part of me is in pain?

2. Where did this pain first take root?

3. How has it shaped my behavior?

4. What lesson is hidden here?

5. What energy do I need to heal this?

The Shadow Mirror
1. What truth am I avoiding?

2. What am I projecting onto others?

3. What belief is keeping me small?

4. What part of me wants to be heard?

5. How can I begin to integrate this part?

The Saboteur Spread
1. What self-sabotaging pattern do I repeat?

2. What triggers it?

3. What do I gain from keeping it alive?

4. What is the cost of holding onto it?

5. What support will help me release it?

When doing these spreads, journal your results. Don't try to rush. If you need to sit with one card for a week, do it. Let it speak. Let it sink in. You don't need to solve everything overnight. Shadow work is slow magic. It's like excavation—you chip away at the stone until the shape inside is revealed.

You can also use tarot for active shadow rituals. Not just reading—but casting.

Let's say you're working through old rage. Pull **The Tower** and **Five of Wands**, place them on your altar, and surround them with black tourmaline and red thread. Write down what you're angry about. Speak it aloud—get it out of your body. Burn the paper in a fire-safe dish. Let the smoke rise like a scream you've finally released.

Or maybe you're grieving something you never got to mourn. Pull **Five of Cups** or **Three of Swords**, place a bowl of water in front of the card, and cry if the tears come. Let the card bear witness. When you're done, pour the water into the earth. Let it carry your sorrow into something that can grow again.

Shadow work can also be about reclaiming power. If you've been silenced, ignored, or told your voice was too much—pull **Queen of Swords**. Light a blue candle. Write a letter you never sent. Stand in front of a mirror and read it to yourself with your whole chest. Then fold the paper, wrap it in red thread, and place it under the card. Let her guard it. Let her bless your voice.

The point isn't to wallow. It's to acknowledge. To integrate. To *stop hiding from yourself.* Because everything you bury will come back stronger. It'll speak through your spells, through your body, through your choices—until you listen.

And the truth is, the parts you're afraid of? The ones you've shoved into the corners of your spirit? They're often the very parts that hold your magic. Your rage? It teaches you what you will and won't allow. Your sorrow? It deepens your compassion. Your fear? It shows you where your edges are—and how to push past them. When you bring these parts into the light, they don't control you anymore. They become your allies.

That's the real gift of shadow work. It's not about cleaning yourself up. It's about making peace with the truth—and becoming whole.

Tarot helps because it's unafraid. It shows you what's *actually* there, not what you want to believe. And the more you work with it in this way, the more honest your magic becomes. You stop casting spells from fear or desperation. You start casting from truth, from clarity, from personal power. You stop avoiding the Devil—and start learning what he can teach you about liberation.

If you're ready to take this further, consider making shadow work a regular part of your magical practice. You don't need to live in it all the time—that's not healthy. But visiting the shadow with intention, with ritual, and with respect will deepen everything else you do.

Here are a few ways to keep the practice alive:

- Pull a "shadow card of the week" and journal on it. Let it guide your reflections.

- When a difficult card shows up in a reading, don't set it aside. Ask, "What part of me needs to hear this?"

- Create a shadow altar with cards, stones, symbols, and offerings tied to your own underworld journey.

- Use the waning moon or dark moon to do deeper inner work with the deck. These are times when the veil between conscious and unconscious is thinner.

And remember—shadow work isn't about becoming someone new. It's about remembering who you've always been beneath the conditioning, the coping, the fear, and the silence.

Let the cards show you the monsters under the bed— and then sit down and ask them what they need. You might be surprised to find they look a lot like you.

ANCESTRAL WORK

If you've ever lit a candle and whispered the name of someone who passed, you already know what it means to practice ancestral work. It's not just about honoring the dead—it's about remembering who you come from, calling back what was lost, and weaving your roots into your ritual. It's not about perfection. It's about presence. And tarot can help guide that presence into something sacred.

In folk magic, conjure, and countless spiritual traditions, working with the ancestors is foundational. It's how we honor bloodlines, chosen kin, cultural lineages, and the spirits who walk with us whether we remember them or not. Ancestral work brings strength, clarity, and healing. It also brings accountability. We don't just inherit blessings—we inherit burdens. And part of our work as magical people is learning how to carry both with grace.

Tarot offers us a way to speak with the dead. It's not just a mirror—it's a mouthpiece. A deck can become a medium, a map, and a sacred bridge between the world of the living and the realm of the beyond. It listens. It answers. It reflects. And it does so without ego or agenda. That's what makes it such a trustworthy tool for ancestral practice.

You don't need a psychic gift to reach out. You just need quiet, intention, and respect. The ancestors don't demand grand gestures—they ask for sincerity. They want to be remembered. They want to be spoken to, not about. And they want to see that their stories live on through your hands.

So how do we bring tarot into ancestral work?

First, begin by creating a space. This could be a formal ancestor altar with photos, offerings, and candles, or it could be something small and simple—a glass of water and a white candle on a shelf. Place the tarot deck at the center, wrapped in cloth or laid atop a piece of fabric or wood that holds significance. Let this be a place where you come to listen.

When you're ready, start with a prayer or invocation. Speak from the heart. Name your known ancestors if you have them. If you don't, that's alright—call in your "beloved dead," your bloodline, your cultural or spiritual lineage, or the wise ones who walk with your soul. Say something like:

"To my ancestors known and unknown, blood and spirit, those who walked before me and made the way—I welcome you. Come close. Guide me. Speak if you will. I am listening."

Then shuffle the cards. Ask a question. Keep it simple. Here are a few examples:

- What message do my ancestors have for me at this time?

- What pattern or burden am I being asked to heal?

- How can I better honor those who came before me?

- What support are my ancestors offering me now?

Pull one to three cards and read them slowly. Don't rush to interpret with your head. Let your body feel the answer. Often, the cards will carry a tone—gentle, urgent, sorrowful, proud. That tone matters just as much as the imagery. If you feel emotion rise, let it. If you feel nothing, trust that too. Spirit doesn't always speak in big signs. Sometimes it shows up as a quiet sense of knowing.

Keep a journal of what you receive. Over time, you may notice patterns. Certain cards may show up frequently in your ancestor readings. For some, **The Hermit** becomes a guide—a solitary elder who walks beside them. Others may often receive **The Six of Cups**, a card soaked in memory and longing. Some ancestors speak through **Judgement**, a call to awaken and rise. Others use **The Empress** to offer comfort, nourishment, and ancestral strength through the feminine line.

You can also use the deck to uncover unresolved issues in your family tree. These can be issues in the recent past that you are aware of or even issues of your distant ancestors that you have no idea even exist. If you're dealing with inherited trauma, generational poverty, cycles of abandonment, addiction, silence—lay the cards and ask:

- What am I carrying that isn't mine?

- What wound runs through my lineage?

- What do my ancestors want me to release?

Be prepared. These spreads can bring up emotions. Grief. Rage. Compassion. And they should. That's the work. You're not just lighting candles—you're shifting energy that may have been stagnant for generations. You're becoming the healer your ancestors didn't have. And you're using the cards not just to *see* the wound, but to *rewrite* the story.

Some people choose to assign specific cards to specific ancestors. You might choose **The Emperor** to represent a grandfather, **The Queen of Pentacles** for a nurturing grandmother, or **The Knight of Swords** for someone who was bold but impulsive. This can be especially helpful if you're doing altar work or creating spirit offerings tied to a particular family member. You can place their card on the altar during prayer, or use it in spellwork when asking for their guidance.

Here's a simple ritual you can try:

Ancestral Message Spread Tools: Tarot deck, white candle, glass of water, journal

1. Light the candle and say
   "I open this space with love and respect. I
   ask for wisdom from my ancestors who walk
   with me."

2. Shuffle the deck while focusing on your breath. Ask:
    "What message do you have for me today?"

3. Pull three cards:

- Card 1: The voice—who is speaking?

- Card 2: The message—what they want you to know

- Card 3: The action—what they want you to do next

4. Sit with the reading. Don't overthink it. Write down what comes through, even if it doesn't make sense yet. Sometimes spirit speaks in riddles that unfold over time.

When you're done, close the space. Say thank you. Snuff the candle. Change the water. These little acts of care matter. The dead notice when you tend to them with consistency.

You can also use tarot in ritual offerings. Say you're preparing food for a feast day, ancestor night, or personal remembrance. Place a card beside the dish that represents what the meal is meant to offer: **The Sun** for celebration, **The Moon** for mystery, **The Star** for guidance, **The Lovers** for reconciliation. These cards act as silent prayers. You don't need to explain them. The spirits understand the language.

If you're walking through grief, tarot can also help you hold the silence. Pull cards that give voice to what you can't speak. Let the cards show you what still lingers in your heart. Light a candle, lay **Five of Cups**, and let your sorrow rise. Lay **Ten of Swords**, and feel the sharpness of loss. Then pull **The Star**, and ask to be guided gently back to light.

Not all ancestors are easy to work with. Some may carry harm, ignorance, or patterns you've had to escape. You are not required to honor those who hurt you. But you can still acknowledge the line, still do healing work, without inviting every spirit in. Use tarot to create boundaries. Ask:

- Which ancestor is safe for me to work with now?

- What protection do I need as I open this path?

- How can I honor my lineage without repeating its harm?

Let the cards guide you toward the allies. And don't be afraid to set limits. Just because someone is blood doesn't mean they get a seat at your altar. Magic is about choice. Choose who you welcome.

For those who don't know their ancestry—whether through adoption, estrangement, or lost records—tarot becomes even more valuable. You can work with your spiritual ancestors. Your magical lineage. The wise ones who walk your path, even if they never knew your name. Ask your deck:

- Who walks with me?

- What legacy am I here to carry forward?

- How can I connect with my spirit lineage?

Pull the cards. Let them speak. You don't have to know the names. You just have to be open. Ancestors aren't bound by paper records. They're bound by love, by energy, by memory. They know who you are. And they're watching.

Ancestral work with tarot isn't a one-time ritual. It's a relationship. The more you show up, the more you'll receive. The more you listen, the clearer the guidance becomes. Over time, your deck will hold not just your own voice, but theirs too.

SIMPLE ANCESTOR RITUAL

Choose a flowering plant that speaks to the spirit of your ancestor—maybe a rose for your grandmother who loved to tend her garden, or marigolds for the uncle who always protected the family. On the day of planting, gather a jar of water, a single white candle, a photo or token of the ancestor, and your tarot deck. Find a quiet patch of soil, and as you dig into the earth, speak aloud the name of the one you're honoring. Place the seedling into the ground, pack the soil gently, and light the candle beside it.

When the moment feels right, pull a single card and lay it face up on the ground beside the plant. Read the card not just with your eyes, but with your heart—see it as a message from your beloved dead, something they want you to know or carry forward. Leave the card in the sunlight for a few moments as an offering, then take it back indoors to place on your ancestor altar or tuck it into your journal. Let the candle burn down as the first blessing upon the plant.

THE TAROT SPELLBOOK

A tarot card is more than a tool for divination—it's a working magical object. You can speak to it, cast with it, and treat it like any other ritual item in your kit. In this chapter, we're going beyond interpretation and into the realm of practice. These are spells. Real ones. Spells you can cast with the cards themselves—no guesswork, no fluff.

When you bring a tarot card into spellwork, you're anchoring the energy of that card into your intention. You're not just calling in an archetype—you're fixing it into place with physical and symbolic reinforcement. The spell becomes layered: candle, card, herbs, spoken word, and spirit, all working in harmony.

You can use a card by placing it on the altar, setting it underneath a working candle, tucking it into a charm bag, or even burying or burning it (photocopies only—don't ruin your deck). Some people create tarot grids, laying several cards in a spread that functions like a magical circuit board. Others just use one strong card as the heart of the working. Either way works. What matters is that the card is charged with your intention.

Below are sample spells for some of the most common needs in magical practice. These can be adjusted to fit your personal style. Use the cards suggested, or swap them for ones that speak more directly to your situation. What matters most is that the energy feels right.

SPELL FOR DRAWING A NEW LOVER

You'll need: The Lovers, Two of Cups, pink candle, rose petals (pink, white or red,), honey, parchment. Dress the candle with oil and sprinkle rose petals around it. Write your desire on parchment and place it beneath the Two of Cups. Lay The Lovers card above the petition. Drizzle a line of honey between the two cards. Light the candle and say:

"Let love come gently, with open hands and a true heart."

Keep the cards and parchment on your altar until the candle has burned out. Bury the parchment and rose petals near your front door or bedroom window. If you live in an apartment you can use a potted plant or burn the paper and release it to the wind.

SPELL FOR BREAKING A BAD HABIT

You'll need: The Devil (reversed), Eight of Cups, black thread, scissors, small mirror Write the habit on a slip of paper. Fold it and place it under The Devil card, laid face down (to signify reversed energy). Tie the mirror with black thread and place it above the Eight of Cups. Speak your intent clearly:

"I leave behind what binds me. I walk forward, free."

Cut the thread. Let the mirror sit face down for one moon cycle. Then break the mirror (safely) and bury the shards far from home.

SPELL FOR PROSPERITY AND STEADY INCOME

You'll need: Ace of Pentacles, Nine of Pentacles, green or yellow candle, cinnamon, five coins Anoint the candle with prosperity oil or olive oil. Sprinkle cinnamon around the base. Place the Ace of Pentacles beneath the candle and the Nine of Pentacles beside your coins. Hold the coins and say:

"May my hands be steady, my harvest rich, my work respected."

Keep the coins in your wallet or near your register if you run a business. Repeat monthly under the waxing moon.

SPELL FOR PHYSICAL HEALING AND STRENGTH

You'll need: Temperance, Four of Swords, white candle, rosemary, blue string, your name or the name of the person you want to comfort or heal. Wrap the name paper in rosemary and tie it with the string. Place it between Temperance and the Four of Swords. Light the candle and say:

"Bring balance to the body, peace to the mind, rest to the bones."

Let the candle burn all the way down, sealing your intention into the space with gentle light. Then take the rosemary bundle and tuck it beneath your pillow for dream-healing, or place it in a sacred corner of your home where it can work quietly until your spirit feels soothed and your healing begins to take root.

SPELL FOR SPIRITUAL PROTECTION

You'll need: tarot cards of Strength and The Star, black candle, salt, garlic skin, iron nail Lay out a ring of salt. Place The Star card at the top and Strength at the bottom. Set the candle and the iron nail in the center. Burn the garlic skin before lighting the candle. Say:

"Let no harm cross my threshold. Let my will stand unbroken."

Use the nail to mark a symbol of protection in wax. Keep the nail near the front door or in a charm bag.

SPELL FOR RECONCILIATION AND EMOTIONAL REPAIR

You'll need: Three of Swords, Two of Cups, pink string, photo or name of the person Write a short apology, confession, or healing statement. The key to this spell working is that you actually have to mean what you say – the apology must be sincere. Something to keep in mind before performing the work. Wrap it with the Two of Cups and their photo using the pink string. Place the Three of Swords below it. Say:

"Let what was broken be softened. Let hearts remember what mattered."

Keep this bundle near a candle for seven days. Then untie it and bury the string. Keep the rest in a sacred place or burn it for closure.

SPELL FOR CAREER GROWTH AND OPPORTUNITY

You'll need: The Magician, Eight of Pentacles, yellow candle, bay leaf (preferably a whole one), pen Write your goal on the bay leaf. Place it under The Magician card. Lay the Eight of Pentacles to the right of the card and light the candle above them. Speak aloud:

"Let my talent be seen. Let doors open. Let work become reward."

Carry the bay leaf in your wallet or burn it to release the energy.

These are starter spells. You can build your own based on the same structure: choose a card that matches the intention, then pair it with physical elements that support the energy—herbs, colors, objects, spoken words. Tarot adds the symbolic charge, helping shape and focus your spell.

Not every working needs multiple cards. Sometimes one is enough. Let's say you want clarity. Pull **Ace of Swords**, place it on your altar, and light a white candle next to it. Say nothing. Just sit and listen. The card speaks.

Tarot spells can be short-term or long-form. You might do a one-night working with quick energy, or you might build a spell that runs over the course of a lunar cycle, with a card draw each week to show your progress. The point is to let the tarot shape the timeline—not just the outcome.

When you're building your own spells, here are a few things to consider:

- **Card choice**: Always match the card's full energy to your intent—not just the keyword. Look at the image, the number, the suit. A card's meaning can shift slightly depending on the context.

- **Elements**: Match the card's suit to herbs, colors, or tools. Cups? Use water, shells, rose. Wands? Use fire, cinnamon, sun oil. Swords? Feathers, wind symbols, lemongrass. Pentacles? Salt, stones, soil.

- **Moon phase**: Add timing for power. Waxing to draw. Waning to release. Full moon to charge. New moon to plant seeds.

- **Outcome**: Be specific. Don't just say "I want love." Say "I want a loving, emotionally available partner who shares my values." The tarot responds to precision.

- **Closure**: Always close your spell intentionally. Snuff candles, bury offerings, clear the cards, thank the spirits. Clean endings matter in magic.

If a card comes up that doesn't seem to match your goal, pay attention. Maybe you're asking for a new relationship and **The Hermit** appears. That might be a sign that the spell should be about inner healing first. Or maybe you're casting for wealth and pull **Four of Pentacles**, telling you to look at where you're hoarding energy or afraid to spend. Use these messages to refine the working. The cards will guide if you listen.

Lastly, trust your results. Not every spell gives you fireworks. Some move slow. Some shift energy in subtle ways first. But if your intention is clear, your will is focused, and the cards are charged properly, the magic will move. Keep a spell journal. Write down what you cast, when, and what happened. Over time, you'll learn your patterns and fine-tune your methods.

You don't need a hundred tools to work effective tarot magic. You just need your deck, a quiet space, and the will to speak clearly. The rest is layers—built by instinct, sharpened by experience. And the cards? They're ready when you are.

SPELL TO DEEPEN YOUR CONNECTION WITH YOUR TAROT CARDS

You'll need:
– Your tarot deck
– A purple or indigo cloth
– A white candle
– A cup of water
– A pinch of dried mugwort or lavender
– Your breath and a quiet space

Begin by spreading the cloth on a flat surface. Set your tarot deck in the center, resting like a heart waiting to be heard. Place the candle above the deck, the cup of water to the right, and the herbs to the left. Sit comfortably before your cards and take three slow breaths, inhaling with intention, exhaling any distraction. Light the candle and say:

"By flame and flow, by leaf and breath,
Reveal your voice, defy all death.
Through image, symbol, thread, and rhyme,
Let card and spirit now align."

Sprinkle the herbs lightly over the cards, just enough to scent the air. Dip your fingers in the water and touch the top card of the deck, saying:

"As water remembers, so shall I.
Speak through me, cards, and never lie."

Shuffle the deck slowly, touching each card as if greeting an old friend. Let your hands learn the feel of them again. When you're ready, pull one card and gaze at it. What emotion stirs? What part of the card pulls at you? Let it speak.

When you're finished, extinguish the candle and wrap your deck in the cloth. Keep it close to you that night—beneath your pillow, beside your bed, or on your altar. Repeat the spell whenever your connection with the cards feels distant. This is how you teach them to trust you—and how you learn to trust them.

ETHICS OF TAROT MAGIC

When you start casting spells with tarot, you're doing more than manipulating symbols. You're shaping energy. You're reaching into the current of fate, will, and spirit and giving it direction. That kind of work deserves a firm foundation—not just in technique, but in ethics.

Every magical path has its own view on what's "right." Some traditions follow strict laws, while others leave it up to personal judgment. But tarot, especially when used in spellcasting, demands you think about what you're doing and why. The cards don't lie. They'll show you what's coming. They'll reflect what's inside you. And if you're not honest with yourself about your motivations, your magic will show it.

Ethics in tarot magic begins with intention. Ask yourself: is this spell meant to control someone, or to empower you? Is it meant to heal a wound, or reopen one that hasn't stopped bleeding? Are you trying to get clarity—or get revenge? The truth matters. Because intention isn't just about words—it's the current that runs under the entire working. You can't trick the cards. They will always read your real desire, no matter what you say out loud.

Consent is another key part of ethical tarot magic. That includes both the cards and the people involved. Reading tarot for someone without their permission, or casting a spell on their behalf without asking, is a spiritual intrusion. Just because you *can* read the cards for someone doesn't mean you should. And just because you want someone to love you, come back, or change their mind, doesn't mean a spell will make it happen—or that it should.

This doesn't mean you can't do spellwork involving other people. What it means is you need to be clear on the difference between influence and interference. A spell to open the door for communication is one thing. A spell to dominate someone's will is another. There's a big difference between asking for clarity and demanding control.

Let's say you're working a reconciliation spell. If you're using cards like **Two of Cups**, **The Lovers**, and **Page of Cups**, and your intention is to heal miscommunication or open space for mutual healing—that's a respectful working. But if you're adding **The Devil** or **The Magician reversed**, and your real goal is to force someone to crawl back whether they want to or not—that's where the ethics get muddy.

In those cases, ask yourself: why do I want this? What do I really hope to gain? And what am I willing to give up to get it?

Magic works best when it aligns with truth. The more you twist your intention, the messier the result. That's not karma in the Hollywood sense. It's just the natural law of energy. What you send out always carries a trace of your spirit with it. If you're casting from desperation, you'll keep pulling desperate outcomes. If you're casting from bitterness, the results might taste as sour as the spell itself.

There's also the issue of privacy and energetic boundaries. If you're pulling cards to spy on someone's feelings, relationship, job, or health without their knowledge, you're stepping into unethical ground. The cards will answer—but the act of asking has consequences. Every time you do it, you're saying, "I believe my need to know outweighs their right to keep it private." That might not bite you the first time, but over time, that kind of magic will isolate you. The more you invade, the more you'll feel watched. Because you are—by the spirits, by the cards, and by the natural flow of balance.

This doesn't mean you can't ask questions about a situation that involves another person. But the question should always bring the focus back to you. Instead of "What is my ex thinking about me?" ask "What do I need to understand about this ending so I can move forward?" That way, the spell becomes an act of healing—not surveillance.

The ethics of tarot magic also extend to how you treat the cards themselves. A tarot deck isn't just a tool— it's a spiritual ally. It holds your energy, your secrets, your spells. Treat it with respect. Cleanse it regularly. Wrap it in cloth. Don't toss it into the bottom of a drawer or leave it coated in wax and ashes. And when you use it in magic, thank it afterward. Just like a candle or a crystal, the cards hold charge—and that charge needs tending.

You don't have to follow anyone else's moral code to practice tarot magic ethically. But you do need to create one of your own—and stick to it. That means being honest with yourself about what kinds of spells you're willing to do, and where you draw the line.

For example:

- Will you cast love spells that name a specific person?

- Are you comfortable doing hexes or bindings?

- Do you believe in baneful magic—and if so, when is it justified?

- Are there situations where you'd cast a spell on someone's behalf without asking them first?

- Are you open to charging for magical work, and if so, how do you ensure fairness?

These aren't questions you answer once and never revisit. They evolve. Your practice will change over time, and so will your ethics. That's healthy. But having a working moral compass helps keep your magic aligned and focused. It also helps you avoid spiritual fallout when something doesn't go the way you planned.

You may also want to include ethical statements in your magical journal or tarot grimoire. This can be a list of personal vows or a simple mission statement like: *"I use tarot only to heal, reveal, and empower. I do not read for others without permission. I use spellwork to support free will, not override it."* This kind of grounding helps you stay clear when the emotions are running high or the situation is messy.

It's also worth saying this: not everyone who practices tarot magic is going to follow ethical guidelines. Some people will lie about their abilities, manipulate others through readings, or use fear to sell spells. If you're serious about this path, you need to learn to spot that behavior early and avoid it. Tarot should never be used to scare, shame, or pressure someone into handing over money, trust, or power. If someone's practice feels exploitative, it probably is.

On the flip side, don't let fear of doing it wrong paralyze you. Ethical magic doesn't mean timid magic. You can be bold, powerful, and assertive without crossing the line. You can cast for love, success, justice, and change—just make sure your spell is honest, your tools are clean, and your spirit is clear.

The goal is to cast in a way that aligns with who you are and what you stand for. Your ethics are your magical backbone. They shape how your spells unfold, how your readings land, and how your spirit feels after the candle burns out.

And if a working leaves you feeling uneasy or sick in the gut, pay attention. That's your magic telling you something was out of alignment. Don't ignore it. Learn from it. Adjust and move forward. Ethical practice doesn't mean perfection. It means awareness. It means responsibility. And it is up to you to pay attention.

TAROT AS A DAILY RITUAL

Some of the most powerful magic doesn't come from full moons or elaborate rituals. It comes from showing up. Lighting a candle, shuffling the cards, and paying attention. That daily contact—the quiet kind—is where the relationship between you and your deck becomes real. Not a performance. Not a prediction. Just presence. This is what daily ritual looks like.

Working with tarot every day doesn't mean pulling a full spread or crafting a spell each morning. It means letting the cards speak to your current energy, your focus, or what needs shifting. The cards become a mirror and a map. They show you where the path is smooth and where it's buckling. And over time, this small daily act builds spiritual discipline.

Start simple. One card a day. That's all it takes. Shuffle your deck in the morning and ask, *"What energy am I working with today?"* or *"What do I need to know to walk in alignment?"* Then draw one card and place it somewhere visible—on your altar, tucked in your journal, or propped against a candle.

Don't overanalyze it. Just take it in. Look at the image. Feel the suit. Let it sit with you while you go about your day. Some days the meaning will be clear. Other days it won't make sense until later, when something clicks into place. That's part of the process. The goal isn't to get it right. The goal is to stay connected.

Evening rituals can go just as deep. Pull a card at night and ask, *"What did I miss today?"* or *"Where did my energy get pulled off track?"* or *"What should I release before resting?"* These questions help you close the loop. They show you where you need to reset, forgive, or let go before the day turns over.

You can also create a three-card rhythm: morning, midday, and night. Start with a focus card in the morning. At noon or when the energy dips, pull another and ask, *"Where am I now?"* At night, draw a final card to ask, *"What did I learn?"* or *"What do I carry forward?"* This practice works especially well during difficult weeks or emotional cycles where things feel unsteady.

Keep a tarot journal. Nothing fancy. Just a notebook or a set of index cards where you record the date, the card, and a few lines about what it meant or how it showed up. Over time, you'll see patterns. You'll notice which cards show up during certain moon phases, emotional states, or seasonal shifts. That's how the tarot becomes a living system—not just something you study, but something you live with.

Tarot can also be woven into daily spellwork and intention-setting. Pull a card and build a micro-spell around it. If **The Magician** appears, light a red candle and state your intention clearly. If **Four of Swords** appears, drink a calming tea and give yourself permission to rest. If **The Chariot** shows up, anoint your feet with oil and set a clear goal for the day.

These little acts of magic build momentum. They create a spiritual rhythm that matches your life, not someone else's ritual calendar. And that's where real connection grows.

You can use tarot to mark time. Pull a card at the start of each week and let it be your theme. Pull one on the new moon to set your intention. Pull another on the full moon to release what no longer serves. Create your own holidays, marked not by the calendar but by your spirit—then let the tarot guide those rites.

It also helps to assign specific times for check-ins. For example, every Sunday night, you might lay three cards: one for what's been, one for what is, and one for what's coming. That simple spread can help you clear old energy, prepare for the week ahead, and stay aligned without waiting for crisis or burnout.

If you use tarot in your magical or devotional work, create a ritual of offering. Light a candle before you shuffle. Place a cup of water or a sprig of herbs beside the deck as a sign of respect. Speak aloud. Say thank you. These small habits make a difference. They turn your deck into more than a tool. They turn it into a companion.

You might also find it useful to create a ritual card of the month. At the start of each month, draw a card and display it on your altar. Let it become a theme. Journal about it. Cast spells that match its energy. Track your dreams and see how that archetype shows up in the unseen. When the month ends, record your reflections and draw again. This practice turns time into a magical spiral. It gives each season a purpose.

Don't get caught up in doing it "right." Some days you'll forget. Some days you won't have the focus. That's fine. Ritual is about rhythm, not perfection. If you show up more often than not, the bond will grow.

The cards will start showing up in dreams. Their messages will start coming before you even shuffle. That's not coincidence. That's connection.

Eventually, your deck becomes an extension of your awareness. You'll think of a card before you pull it. You'll know when it's time to rest, time to act, time to cut cords—because the cards have taught you how to listen.

Daily ritual with tarot isn't about being mystical 24/7. It's about presence. It's about spiritual maintenance. It's about checking in before everything falls apart. And the more you do it, the more the deck becomes part of your nervous system. You breathe, you shuffle, you know.

DEITY AND SPIRIT WORK WITH TAROT

Working with deities, saints, and spirits is one of the oldest forms of magic there is. Long before people were writing spells in books or naming the four elements, they were lighting candles for gods, whispering to the dead, and leaving offerings at trees, crossroads, and altars. That part of the craft doesn't change. What changes is how we speak to those forces—and tarot can be one of the most direct ways to start the conversation.

You can use tarot in spirit work in a few different ways. It can act as a medium—a way for spirits or deities to speak back to you. It can be used in devotional rituals as an offering or focal point. Or it can help clarify which spirits are with you, what they want, and how best to work with them. The cards give structure to an otherwise invisible dialogue. They become a shared language between you and whatever force you're calling in.

Start with who you're working with. Maybe it's a known deity—Hecate, Brigid, Ogun, the Virgin of Guadalupe. Maybe it's a familiar ancestor or a saint. Maybe it's a local land spirit, a house guardian, or a nameless force that shows up in your dreams. Whatever the case, you need to treat the relationship with respect. This isn't about casting demands into the wind and waiting for results. It's about building trust, consistency, and a working partnership.

Before you ask a question, make sure the space is set. That means cleansing. That means focus. That means offerings. A simple glass of water, a candle, a pinch of incense. Speak aloud. Call the spirit or deity by name. State your intention clearly. Something like: "I come with clean hands and clear purpose. I ask [Name] to join me. Speak through the cards if you will. Show me what I need to know."

Shuffle with purpose. Keep your focus on the connection. You're not just pulling cards for fun—you're opening a channel. Let the cards be part of that. Let them speak.

Start simple. Ask:

- What message do you have for me today?

- How can I deepen my relationship with you?

- What offering would you like at this time?

- What part of my path are you guiding now?

Pull one to three cards. Sit with them. Don't jump to a book definition. Use the deck you normally work with, or one that's been consecrated specifically for spiritual work. Over time, you may find certain cards become signatures—specific to a spirit or deity. You might start pulling **The High Priestess** every time Hecate's energy is strong. Or **Strength** when a particular saint wants to come forward. These patterns matter. Write them down. Over time, they become part of how you recognize spiritual presence when it shows up unannounced.

You can also lay a full spread in devotional space. Use one card to represent the deity or spirit, one for your role in the relationship, one for what they're offering, and one for what they expect from you. You can also pull cards to track progress over time, especially if you're walking through a devotional cycle, offering novenas, or working through a set of rituals tied to the spirit in question.

Some practitioners assign specific cards to different deities, saints, or spirits. There's no universal chart for this, and honestly, there shouldn't be. These assignments come through relationship, not memorization. Still, some patterns are common:

- **The High Priestess**: Hecate, Isis, Cerridwen, any dark goddess or keeper of hidden knowledge

- **The Empress**: Mother Mary, Brigid, Venus, Yemaya

- **The Emperor**: Zeus, Ogun, Saint Joseph, or the divine masculine as protector and builder

- **The Magician**: Hermes, Thoth, trickster spirits, or any being that teaches magic and manifestation

- **The Moon**: spirits of the dead, shadow gods, dream guides, and spirits who come through altered states

- **Judgement**: ancestral guides, gatekeepers, or messenger spirits from the other side

- **The Lovers**: Aphrodite, Eros, saints tied to love and union, or spirits who aid in matters of the heart

You can create your own spirit deck, where each card has been personally linked to a being you've worked with. Write their name on an index card and store it with your notes. Over time, when a card repeats, you'll know who's speaking. This doesn't need to be complex. It just needs to be consistent.

Tarot also works well when building or maintaining altars. Place a card that represents your spirit or deity directly on the altar. Let it serve as a visual and energetic anchor. Change the card when the energy shifts. For example, you might use **The Star** during a period of spiritual healing and shift to **The Chariot** when you need action or protection. The card becomes part of the offering. It says, "I see you. I remember. I'm still here."

You can also use the cards to cast a circle or mark sacred space when working with spirits. Lay four cards—one in each direction—based on what energies need to be called in. Maybe you place **The Tower** in the South to burn away interference, or **The Moon** in the West to open the psychic gate, **The Magician** in the East to focus intention, and **The Empress** in the North to ground and protect. This becomes your spirit circle. You've built it not with chalk or salt, but with symbols that move energy.

When working with spirits who don't speak in clear language—especially land spirits or household spirits—tarot gives them a way to communicate. You might place a small offering bowl and candle in a corner of your home, then leave your deck nearby. Once a week, ask:

- Is there anything you need?

- Are you at peace?

- Is there anything I should know about this space?

Pull one card. Let the image and the suit speak. A **Five of Swords** may show conflict or unrest. A **Ten of Pentacles** could mean the spirit feels rooted and calm. A reversed card may suggest stagnation or disrespect. Adjust your space and offerings accordingly.

One important note: not every spirit wants to work with tarot. Some may prefer other methods—dreams, trance, prayer, offerings, or pure intuition. Respect that. Tarot isn't the only language, and forcing it where it doesn't belong won't get you clear results. Ask first. Use divination to confirm. Be flexible.

You can also use tarot as a filter when spirit communication feels overwhelming or unclear. Say you've had multiple dreams, strange signs, or unexplained sensations, and you're not sure what's coming through. Sit quietly, cleanse your space, and ask:

- Who is trying to reach me?

- Is this energy for my highest good?

- What do they want?

- What is the best way to respond?

If you're dealing with trickster energy, deception, or spirits that aren't being upfront, tarot will usually call it out fast. Cards like **Seven of Swords**, **The Moon**, or **The Devil** often appear when something isn't what it seems. Take those as signs to pause and reassess. You don't owe your energy to every spirit that shows up. That's what boundaries are for.

Tarot can also assist in offering gratitude. After a successful working or a clear sign, pull a card and offer it with purpose. Light a candle, lay down the card, and say aloud:

"Thank you for your guidance. This card is laid in your honor."

Let it sit on the altar for a full day, then return it to the deck after you've acknowledged the connection. These gestures keep the relationship strong.

Spirit work also requires spiritual hygiene. Cleanse your deck regularly, especially if you're using it in mediumship or devotional work. Smoke, salt, moonlight, or prayer all work. Keep a separate deck if you do a lot of ancestor or spirit-based readings. Let that deck hold the charge, and treat it like any sacred object—wrapped, blessed, and respected. If you ever feel off after a reading, trust it.

Yemaya as the Empress card

Zeus as the Emperor card

YOUR TAROT GRIMOIRE

A tarot grimoire is more than a notebook full of definitions. It's not just a cheat sheet or a quick reference. It's a record of your lived experience with the cards. It's where your readings, your spells, your spreads, and your insights come together in one place. Over time, it becomes one of the most personal magical tools you own.

Anyone can buy a tarot book. But your grimoire is built by your hands, shaped by your rituals, and written in your voice. It holds your patterns, your breakthroughs, and your process. When you open it, you're not looking up someone else's idea of what a card means. You're remembering what *you* learned when you pulled that card during a heartbreak, a healing, or a spell that finally worked.

Start by choosing a format that works for how you think and move. Some people use spiral notebooks. Others keep three-ring binders so they can rearrange pages. Some use sketchbooks or digital folders with sections. It doesn't need to be pretty. It just needs to be functional. Your grimoire is a tool, not a coffee table showpiece.

Begin with the basics: one page (or more) for each card. Write the name of the card at the top. Leave space for notes to grow over time. You don't have to fill everything in at once. Start with your first impressions. The imagery. The feeling it gives you. Then add key meanings as you work with the card in different contexts.

Write down how it shows up in spells. What happens when you place it on your altar? What kind of energy does it hold in a protection working versus a love working? Which spirits respond to it? What happens when you dream about it? Does it change its tone when paired with another suit?

Your grimoire should reflect these layers. Don't just write "The Magician means skill and manifestation." Write: "Pulled The Magician during new moon spell—charged my will fast, worked quickly, lots of energy. Needed to ground afterward. Associated it with cinnamon, red candle, and verbal incantations. Strong under Mercury hour."

That's the kind of note you come back to months later and say, "Right. I remember what that felt like." That's what makes it magic.

You can include sketches or symbols. You can press herbs between the pages. You can track how certain cards feel during specific seasons or under certain moon phases. If a card always shows up when you're sick, tired, or out of sync, mark that down. These are your tells—your personal signs. Books won't teach you those. Experience will.

Your tarot grimoire can also include:

- **Readings journal**: Keep a running list of daily draws, weekly spreads, and ritual readings. Include the date, cards pulled, your question, and what happened afterward.

- **Spells and rituals**: Write out your tarot-based spells in full detail. Include the setup, card choice, moon phase, and outcome.

- **Spirit communications**: Track messages received through the cards from ancestors, deities, or guides. Record which cards act as signatures for which spirits.

- **Custom spreads**: Whenever you create a new spread that works, write it down. Include a diagram or layout if needed. Note how well it read and what kind of situation it suited.

- **Symbols and associations**: Track how you personally interpret numbers, colors, directions, or elements in the tarot. Over time, these meanings may change. That's fine—record the evolution.

You can divide the book by suits, by themes, or by type of working. Some people keep one grimoire for spellcasting and another for divination. Some keep a messy working book and a clean copy once patterns emerge. The structure should support your practice—not hinder it. Don't let perfection stop you from putting ink to page.

This isn't just about recording what the cards say. It's about recording what you *did* with them—how the energy moved, what happened, what worked, and what didn't. That kind of documentation is rare in magical books, and it's one of the most powerful tools you can give yourself. Your grimoire becomes proof. A living archive of results.

Eventually, your grimoire becomes your teacher. You'll flip through it after a year and start to notice cycles. You'll see that **The Hermit** always shows up before a breakthrough, or that **Nine of Swords** always lands before a confrontation you didn't want to have. You'll see which cards move spells fast, which ones lag, and which ones never show up at all unless something big is shifting. These are personal mysteries—and your grimoire is where they unfold.
You can also include failures. Not every spell works. Not every reading lands. Sometimes you misread a card, misplace a candle, or cast from a place of desperation. Write that down. Not to shame yourself—but to learn. Write what you felt, what you did, and what you'd do differently next time. That's the kind of honesty that turns magical theory into magical skill.

As your practice deepens, you might add sections for elemental correspondences, deity associations, or planetary influences. You might build ritual blueprints based on spreads that have worked in the past. You might even start creating your own deck, one sketch or symbol at a time, based on how the cards feel to *you* and how they've moved in your life.

Don't be afraid to contradict yourself. You might write one year that **The Fool** felt like freedom and the next year say he felt like carelessness. That's fine. The cards shift. So do you. The point of the grimoire isn't to trap the meanings in stone. It's to track how the symbols grow in your hands.

Protect your grimoire like you would any other sacred object. Keep it close. Don't lend it out. Don't let it gather dust. Visit it often. Add to it after each major reading or ritual. Let it stay messy until you need it to be clean. Let it be a place where the personal and magical collide without pretense.

Over time, this book will become something no one else could ever write—not because of how it's worded, but because of how it's lived.

When you reach for your deck, reach for the grimoire too. They belong together. The deck will speak. The grimoire will remember. And between the two, you'll never be working blind. One is the voice of spirit, the other the record of its wisdom. Your cards will whisper what needs to be known, but your grimoire will catch it, hold it, and shape it into something you can return to again and again. Use both, and your magic becomes not just intuitive, but remembered, refined, and rooted in time.

TIPS FOR ORGANIZING YOUR TAROT JOURNAL OR GRIMOIRE

Write it down while the cards are still warm. Don't wait until the moment passes or the reading fades. Keep your journal close when you pull cards—whether for yourself or someone else. The impressions, gut feelings, and stray symbols mean more in the moment than they ever will an hour later. Your grimoire should be a living thing, not a scrapbook of afterthoughts.

Use symbols, not just words. Let your journal speak in the language of magic. Doodle the suits, trace the phases of the moon, or press in a leaf from the walk you took before your reading. A tarot journal isn't just for documentation—it's for enchantment. Let it look and feel like the spellbook it is.

Divide by purpose, not by date. Don't trap your grimoire in calendar pages. Group your entries by spreads, by themes, by clients, or by questions. Keep a section for daily pulls, another for spells, and maybe one just for dreams. Your tarot work doesn't follow linear time—your journal shouldn't either.

Mark what matters most. Use ribbons, bookmarks, tags, or old scraps of cloth to flag important pages. If a reading blew your mind, changed your course, or confirmed a spell—mark it. Your future self will thank you. The grimoire is both a trail and a treasure map.

Review it like a sacred text. Don't just write and forget. Flip back often. Look at old readings with new eyes. Patterns will emerge, cycles will reveal themselves, and cards that once confused you will speak with clarity. A well-used tarot grimoire is a mirror of your own unfolding magic—tend to it like you would a garden of omens.

ADVANCED TAROT SPELL ARCHITECTURE

By the time you've worked with tarot long enough, the cards stop being just symbols and start becoming tools—tools that don't just answer questions, but shape outcomes. You stop thinking of spells as individual actions and start seeing them as systems. This chapter is about building those systems. Not just a single card on a candle, but full layouts with movement, phases, and purpose. Advanced tarot spellwork is about structure, rhythm, and depth.

Think of it like building a house. A quick spell is a single room—a place to go when you need something specific. Advanced spell architecture is the whole house, from foundation to chimney. It involves timing, layering, and long-form intention. It's not harder. It just asks more of you—more thought, more care, and more presence.

The first step is deciding what kind of structure the spell needs. Some goals are simple. You want to attract love, remove negativity, open the way for prosperity. A single card with a few supporting elements might be enough. But when the goal is layered—such as reclaiming power after trauma, shifting a long-standing situation, or initiating a major life change—you need more than a spark. You need architecture.

That means choosing your cards deliberately. Not just what they represent, but how they function together. Each card becomes a component. One card might be the ignition point. Another might act as an amplifier. One might be the block that needs to be released. Another holds the goal. You're not just reading cards anymore—you're *building* with them.

Let's say you're creating a working to end a toxic relationship pattern and call in something better. You might choose:

- **Eight of Cups** as the card of release

- **The Tower** to break the cycle at its root

- **The Star** for healing

- **The Lovers** for calling in a new, aligned connection

That's not a reading. That's a construction. Each card holds a piece of the spell. You're moving from one to the next like rungs on a ladder. You could place these cards in a line from left to right—past to future. Or build them into a circle, returning the energy inward. Or shape them into a cross to represent the breaking of an old pattern and the anchoring of a new one. The layout matters. The direction matters. The order of energy matters.

Once your card structure is laid, the second layer is correspondence.

This is where you choose the herbs, oils, colors, moon phase, and planetary hour to match the work. If you're using **The Tower**, don't do it under a calm Libra moon unless your goal is to ease into change. If you're going for a hard break, you might choose a waning moon in Scorpio or Mars hour on a Tuesday. Layer the elements intentionally. Let's build a long-form spell using this structure.

SPELL TO BREAK A GENERATIONAL PATTERN AND CLAIM SPIRITUAL AUTHORITY

Time Frame: Seven-day working
Cards Needed: Ten of Swords, The Tower, Judgement, The Magician
Tools:

- Black candle (for banishing)

- White candle (for clarity and spiritual sovereignty)

- Salt and graveyard dirt (to honor the dead and clear the path)

- Small mirror (to reflect the self)

- Pen and paper (to write the inherited pattern)

- String (to bind and release)

- Personal item (a token that connects you to your bloodline or chosen lineage)

Day 1:

Set the space. Cleanse with smoke and salt. Lay the Ten of Swords. Place your personal item in front of it. Write out the pattern that keeps repeating—what was passed down, what you've carried, what you no longer accept. Fold the paper and place it beneath the card. Light the black candle and say with intention: *"This ends with me. I name it. I face it. I let it fall."* Let the candle burn for 30 minutes. Snuff it. Leave everything in place.

Day 2:

Add The Tower to the layout. Sprinkle a line of salt and graveyard dirt around both cards, and maintain concentration. Light the black candle again and say: *"Let it break. Let it burn. Let it never return."* Tear the paper in three pieces and bury it at the edge of your yard or beneath a heavy stone. Snuff the candle. Leave the cards in place.

Day 3:

Place Judgement in the center of the working. Now light both the black and white candles. Speak the names of your ancestors or those whose energy this spell is tied to. If you don't know their names, speak to them anyway. The Universe knows who you mean. Say: *"Rise clean. Rise clear. Rise free. Rise for me."* Use the mirror to reflect the cards and the flames. Let it show you what's changed. Write any dreams or impressions.

Day 4–6:

Each day, light the white candle only. Place The Magician on your altar. Begin crafting a statement of power in your mind—something to the effect of: *"I claim the right to create. I claim the power to choose. My magic begins where my pain ends and I reclaim it now."* Repeat this aloud each day. Wrap the personal item in string and hold it in your dominant hand. Feed the spell with your voice.

Day 7:
Close the spell. Unwrap the string. Place The Magician card and the personal item on your altar permanently. Thank the spirits who walked with you. Pour water into the soil as a sign of release. Journal everything.

That's one example. A full seven-day working built from cards, layers, intention, and action. The more complex the goal, the more structure your spell needs. Some spells work like lightning. Others work like planting a tree. Know the difference.

You can also use tarot to layer spells in phases—what some call "stair-step work." Let's say you're working a long-haul prosperity spell. You might break it into three phases:

1. **Foundation phase:** Use cards like **Four of Pentacles**, **The Hierophant**, or **King of Pentacles**. Cast to stabilize income, reduce leaks, and build discipline.

2. **Growth phase:** Shift to **Six of Pentacles**, **Seven of Pentacles**, and **The Empress**. Cast to increase income, draw in support, or manifest new opportunities.

3. **Sovereignty phase:** Use **Nine of Pentacles**, **The Magician**, or **Queen of Pentacles**. Cast to maintain, protect, and grow your wealth on your terms.

Each phase can last a week, a lunar cycle, or as long as needed. The key is to let each card serve as a focus point for that chapter of the work.

Don't forget magical timing. Advanced tarot spell architecture benefits from planetary hours and moon phases. Working with **The Moon** card during a waning Pisces moon will feel very different than casting with it during a full moon in Cancer. The suit of the card, the spell intention, and the astrological moment all speak to each other. The more you learn to listen, the more power you'll be able to direct.

You can also build magical grids with cards. Picture a four-card compass:

- North: What grounds this spell

- South: What drives it forward

- East: What needs to be spoken or clarified

- West: What needs to be released or washed clean

Place a fifth card in the center as the core intention. This layout becomes the anchor of your spell. Surround it with herbs, candles, or charms as needed. Cards can also be used in mirrored pairings:

- One card facing up: what you are calling in

- One card facing down: what must be banished or broken

Place these cards under your working candle. As the wax melts, imagine the energy of the upright card expanding while the reversed card dissolves. When the candle finishes, burn or bury the reversed card (photocopy) and keep the upright card on your altar. In all of this, remember: clarity first, then power. If you don't know exactly what you're casting for, the spell will run wild. Use spreads to clarify your desire before you even begin. Lay three cards:

- Card 1: What do I *think* I want?

- Card 2: What is the true root of the desire?

- Card 3: What will the likely outcome be if I cast for this?

Let the answers shape the spell. Change course if needed. Refine the working. Tarot doesn't just help cast—it helps *plan*.

As you move into this level of spellwork, keep records. Document the full structure: what cards were used, what phases, what correspondences, and what outcomes. This kind of journaling turns spellcasting into magical architecture. You start to see which combinations are repeatable. You start to identify where your process thrives—and where it gets sloppy.

Advanced doesn't mean flashy. It means focused. It means layered, but not overcomplicated. Every part of the spell should serve the intention. Don't throw in six cards if three will do. Don't add herbs or oils that don't match the goal just to fill the space. This isn't busywork. It's construction. You're building something that's meant to hold weight.

And the cards? They know how to carry it. If you know how to build.

MORE TAROT SPELLS

The following spells are designed for deeper work, long-term impact, and layered energy. Each one uses multiple tarot cards as magical anchors, with detailed instructions for timing, tools, setup, and activation. These are not light spells. They're built for practitioners ready to move energy with precision and responsibility.

BINDING A TOXIC INFLUENCE

Cards: The Devil, Eight of Swords, Justice (reversed)
Tools: Black ribbon, poppet or name paper, black candle, banishing oil, iron nail, rosemary, petition paper

Write the name of the person or situation you want to bind on a small piece of paper or a cloth poppet. Lay down The Devil to represent control, the Eight of Swords for limitation, and Justice reversed for imbalance or wrongdoing. Dress the black candle with banishing oil and surround it with dried rosemary. Place the poppet or name paper in the center of the three cards. Wrap it tightly with the black ribbon as you say:

"By the Devil's chain and the blindfold's hold,
Let your reach be stopped, let your actions fold.
What you cast out shall now rebound,
Your harm restrained, your voice unbound."

Drive the iron nail through the bundle to seal the spell. Burn the candle beside it until it burns down completely. Bury the bundle far from your home, or store it in a locked box until the influence ends. Cleanse your space afterward with rosemary smoke or saltwater.

OPENING THE ROAD TO OPPORTUNITY

Cards: The Chariot, Ace of Pentacles, Three of Wands
Tools: Orange candle, road opener oil, bay leaf, carnelian or citrine, crossroads dirt (optional), petition paper

Lay The Chariot at the base of your workspace to symbolize momentum. Above it, place the Ace of Pentacles for new material opportunities, and the Three of Wands to call in expansion. Anoint the candle with road opener oil. Write your specific opportunity—job, move, project—on the bay leaf and place it beneath the Ace of Pentacles. Arrange crossroads dirt and your chosen stone around the cards. Light the candle and say:

"Let roads open wide, let blocks fall away,
Let chance and choice align today.
I walk forward with will, with skill, with speed—
Every door I need now opens to me."

Burn the bay leaf at the end of the ritual. Carry the stone with you as a charm. Repeat this working at the new moon or on a Wednesday during Mercury hour for stronger movement.

HEALING FROM PAST LOVE

Cards: Three of Swords, Six of Cups (reversed), Temperance
Tools: Pink and blue candle, rose petals, lavender oil, a small dish of water, your own name paper

Create a circle with rose petals. Place the Three of Swords on your left, the reversed Six of Cups in the center, and Temperance on your right. These cards together show the full arc: heartbreak, release of the past, and emotional healing.

Write your full name on a small piece of paper. Place it under Temperance, then drip three drops of lavender oil into the water dish. Light both candles and say:

"What's behind me stays behind.
Old ache and longing, I unwind.
Heart be whole, and soul be clear—
The pain departs, the path is near."

Wash your hands in the water, then pour it outside to release the emotion. Keep Temperance on your altar until your heart feels lighter. Don't try to force it. This could take days, weeks, or months. You will know when it is time to return to card to the deck. Tip: print out the card so that your deck isn't missing a card.

CALLING IN CREATIVE FLOW

Cards: The Star, Page of Wands, Ace of Cups
Tools: Yellow candle, cinnamon, orange peel, watercolors or colored pens, quartz point, blank journal page

Set The Star at the top of your space as your inspiration. Below that, place the Page of Wands and Ace of Cups side by side to represent creative spark and emotional outpouring. Sprinkle cinnamon and orange peel across the cards to activate joy and clarity.

Light the yellow candle and place the quartz at the bottom of the layout. Then hold your journal open and say:

"From spark to flame, from seed to bloom,
Let muse arrive and clear the room.
By wand and cup and sacred star,
Inspiration flow from near and far."

Draw or write freely for fifteen minutes. Let whatever comes move through you without judgment. Repeat this spell whenever you feel creatively blocked.

WARDING AGAINST GOSSIP AND MANIPULATION

Cards: Seven of Swords, Queen of Swords, Five of Wands
Tools: Mirror, white string, alum powder or slippery elm, silver candle, garlic skin, small pouch

Place the mirror at the center of your workspace. Lay the Seven of Swords to the left, Queen of Swords at the top, and Five of Wands to the right. The Seven reveals deception, the Five protects from conflict, and the Queen's sword cuts through the lies with sharp clarity and precision.

Write your name on a strip of paper and wrap it with alum powder or slippery elm bark to stop gossip. Imagine the gossip beginning to fade away with every letter you write. Tie it with white string and place it beside the Queen of Swords. Light the silver candle and burn the garlic skin for added protection. Say:

"Tongues that twist and words that sting,
Fall silent now beneath my wing.
Your tricks return, your slander end—
I call on truth that does not bend."

Place the mirror face-outward near your front door to reflect harmful energy, which, as many know, is also an element of feng shui. Carry the tied pouch in your bag or pocket for ongoing protection.

STRENGTHENING SELF-TRUST

Cards: The High Priestess, Strength, Two of Swords
Tools: Indigo candle, mugwort, tiger's eye, bowl of water, mirror, your written affirmation

Lay the High Priestess at the top of your altar to call in deep knowing. Below her, place Strength to represent courage and inner mastery. Lay the Two of Swords at the base to break through self-doubt and indecision. Sprinkle a pinch of mugwort over the Strength card to sharpen spiritual confidence.

Light the indigo candle. Sit facing the mirror with the cards in front of you and the tiger's eye stone resting in your non-dominant hand. Write an affirmation that claims your authority, such as:

"I trust myself. I know what I know. My spirit speaks, and I listen."

Read it aloud, staring directly into the mirror. Then dip your fingertips in the water and anoint your temples and chest. Say:

"No voice but mine within this space.
No shadow doubt shall take my place.
By strength and sight and inner flame,
I cast self-trust in my own name."

Keep the tiger's eye with you during decision-making or meditation. Burn the candle nightly for three nights, repeating the affirmation aloud.

DRAWING A MENTOR OR GUIDE

Cards: The Hierophant, King of Wands, Page of Pentacles
Tools: Brown candle, calendula, rosemary, bay leaf, yellow thread, your written request

Lay out the Hierophant as your beacon—calling in wisdom and tradition. To his right, place the King of Wands to represent a bold and experienced guide, someone who won't steer you the wrong way. On his left, the Page of Pentacles—your willingness to learn.

Dress the candle with rosemary and calendula petals for attraction and spiritual support.

On the bay leaf, write what kind of guidance you're seeking: teacher, business mentor, spiritual elder, or wise companion. You might even do this during a meditation session to help call upon the spirit you need. Wrap it in yellow thread while saying:

"Let wisdom walk where I can see.
A guide appears, aligned with me.
By leaf and fire, mentor come—
May truth and skill beat like a drum."

Burn the candle and keep the bay leaf bundle near your altar until someone fitting crosses your path. If you meet a teacher or elder during the next moon cycle, revisit this layout and give thanks.

RELEASING ANCESTRAL SHAME

Cards: Five of Cups, Death, Judgement
Tools: Black and white candles, graveyard dirt (or earth from family land), charcoal, myrrh resin, your family name written on paper

Begin by laying the Five of Cups and Death side by side. These cards represent inherited sorrow and the need to sever ties with shame-based legacy. Place Judgement above them to guide the spirit into renewal. Anoint both candles—black for the past, white for clarity—with graveyard dirt if available.

Write your family surname on a piece of paper. Fold it and place it beneath the Death card. Light the black candle and burn myrrh on charcoal. Speak aloud:

"I name what has been carried too long—
Secrets, blame, what was done wrong.
I send it back through ash and bone,
No longer mine, I stand alone."

Then light the white candle and say:

"But what was wise, I call to me.
What was sacred, I set free.
I rise from line, from root, from flame—
And walk unburdened, without shame."

Burn or bury the name paper after the working. Leave Judgement on your altar for three days to invite spiritual closure.

CLAIMING FINANCIAL POWER

Cards: King of Pentacles, Nine of Pentacles, Ace of Pentacles
Tools: Gold or green candle, cinnamon stick, pyrite, basil, bank statement or business plan

Lay the King of Pentacles at the top of your layout—he rules over finances and stability. Below him, place the Nine of Pentacles to claim independence and luxury. Anchor the spell with the Ace of Pentacles at the base—your seed of wealth.

Dress the candle in cinnamon powder. Place your bank statement or business paper under the Ace of Pentacles. Arrange basil leaves and pyrite around the layout. Light the candle and say:

"Let wealth arrive in ways I choose,
Through work I honor, skills I use.
Not taken, begged, or born of greed—
But earned with power, and planted like seed."

Sit with the layout and visualize your finances growing. Speak aloud any specific financial goal. Burn the candle for nine minutes a night for nine nights. Keep the basil leaf in your wallet for ongoing influence.

BANISHING LINGERING SPIRIT ENERGY

Cards: The Moon, Ten of Swords, The World
Tools: Black salt, white candle, iron key, bell, lemon peel, protective oil, name or description of energy (if known)

Lay The Moon card on the left to represent the spirit's shadowy presence. Ten of Swords in the center to finalize the cut. The World on the right to seal and close the door for good. Create a circle of black salt around the cards.

Write down the name of the lingering spirit or describe the energy on a piece of paper. Anoint the paper with protective oil. Set the iron key and lemon peel on top of it.

Light the candle and say:

"What lingers here must now depart.
Your thread is cut, I close my heart.
By key and peel and bell's sharp ring,
Your time is done. Leave everything."

Ring the bell once in each direction—north, south, east, west. Then burn the paper safely and scatter the ashes outside your home, at the base of a tree or crossroads.

Bury the lemon peel near your front door. Keep The World on your altar for seven days as a barrier.

DREAMING TRUE: A SPELL FOR REVEALING HIDDEN TRUTHS IN SLEEP

Cards: The Moon, The High Priestess, Nine of Swords
Tools: Blue candle, mugwort, amethyst, a white cloth, your pillowcase, bowl of spring water

Begin by laying out the cards in a triangle with The Moon at the top, The High Priestess to the left, and the Nine of Swords to the right. This spread holds the shape of a gateway—one that invites truth from the unconscious. Sprinkle a small pinch of mugwort around the layout to activate the gateway between waking and dreaming. Light the blue candle and place the bowl of spring water beneath the triangle of cards. Hold the amethyst in your dominant hand and whisper your question or concern over the water. Then dip your fingers in the water and anoint your forehead. Say aloud:

"Dreams reveal what day conceals.
Let what's hidden now unseal.
By Moon and veil and silent night,
Show me truth and give me sight."

Place the amethyst inside your pillowcase and fold the white cloth over the cards to hold the spell while you sleep. In the morning, journal what you remember. If the dreams are unclear, repeat for three consecutive nights. Burn a fresh blue candle each night and refresh the bowl of water.

SPELL TO CUT EMOTIONAL CORDS
THAT NO LONGER SERVE

Cards: Eight of Cups, Queen of Swords, The Devil
Tools: Black candle, cord or red thread, a photo or name paper, lemon oil, scissors

Lay the Eight of Cups above the Queen of Swords, with The Devil facing both from the opposite side. These cards together represent emotional detachment, clarity, and release from unhealthy attachment. Dress the black candle with lemon oil to sever and purify. Tie the cord or red thread loosely around the name paper or photo of the person or situation you're releasing. Light the candle and speak your full name aloud. Hold the cord in both hands and say:

"This thread is not mine to keep.
What once was strong now falls asleep.
Bound no more by guilt or pain,
I walk alone. I break this chain."

Cut the cord and allow it to fall from your hands. Burn the cut pieces in a fire-safe bowl if possible. Let the candle burn down completely. Store the Queen of Swords on your altar for seven days to reinforce your clarity.

Remember, for cord cutting spells to work you have to truly be ready to let go of the past and the feelings attached to the situation.

Spell to Awaken and Strengthen Intuition

Cards: Page of Cups, The Star, Two of Pentacles
Tools: Purple candle, jasmine tea, silver coin, a mirror, lavender, journal

Lay the Page of Cups in the center to open the channel. Place The Star above it as a celestial guide and the Two of Pentacles below to balance intuition with discernment. Brew a cup of jasmine tea and dress the purple candle with lavender. Light the candle and sit with the cards, holding the silver coin in your palm. Place the mirror where you can look into it, and say:

"Let insight rise from gentle stream,
Not dreamless sleep, but sacred dream.
I ask not noise, but voice within—
To speak with truth through breath and skin."

Sip the tea slowly, allowing the herbs and candle to attune you. When finished, close your eyes and focus inward. Let the mirror and cards reflect what comes. Record everything in your journal—images, sensations, impressions. Repeat weekly to strengthen your inner ear.

SPELL TO SHIFT A STUBBORN SITUATION

Cards: Five of Pentacles, The Tower, Six of Swords
Tools: Orange candle, clove oil, lodestone or magnet, parchment, bay leaf, bowl of salt water

The Five of Pentacles goes on the left to represent stagnation and hardship. The Tower stands at the center to break the pattern. The Six of Swords faces forward, drawing energy into resolution. Dress the orange candle in clove oil and set it on top of a small plate of salt water to cleanse and cut through blockages.

Write the situation you want to shift on parchment and place it beneath The Tower card. Lay the bay leaf across the top and say:

"Stuck no more, I break this knot.
Let it shift, whether fair or not.
By fire's will and clove's command,
I move the stuck with steady hand."

Light the candle and place the lodestone beside the Six of Swords to draw change. Let the candle burn for a full hour. Burn the bay leaf and bury the ashes off your property. Keep the lodestone on your altar until movement is felt.

SPELL FOR STRENGTHENING
PERSONAL BOUNDARIES

Cards: Nine of Wands, Queen of Pentacles, Justice
Tools: White candle, black tourmaline, a circle of salt, petition paper, rosemary, clear bowl of water

Form a small circle of salt and place the three cards within: Nine of Wands at the top for protection, Queen of Pentacles to the right for grounded strength, and Justice to the left for firm, fair boundary-setting. Write a petition stating your boundary clearly: "I choose where my energy flows," or "I do not accept [specific intrusion]." If the intrustion is a specific person, you can always write your petition on top of their photograph.

Anoint the white candle with rosemary oil or fresh leaves. Place the black tourmaline at the bottom of the circle. Light the candle and hold your hands over the layout, saying:

"I know my shape. I name my line.
This space is sacred, wholly mine.
None may cross without consent—
And what I will, shall not be bent."

Drop a pinch of salt into the water bowl to seal the spell. Place the tourmaline beside your front door or under your bed. Burn the candle for nine minutes a day for three days, repeating the affirmation aloud.

SPELL TO SILENCE A TROUBLE-MAKER

Cards: Five of Swords, Queen of Swords, Seven of Wands
Tools: Black candle, slippery elm bark or powder, alum, name paper or photo, small jar, black thread, pins

Lay the Five of Swords at the center—this represents someone who causes discord through manipulation or malice. Place the Queen of Swords above it to call in sharp truth and mental clarity. The Seven of Wands faces outward at the base to shield and defend your energy.

Write the full name of the troublemaker on a slip of paper. Sprinkle slippery elm and alum across it. Fold it away from you and wrap it in black thread until tightly bound. Push three pins through the bundle— one for the mouth, one for the hands, one for the heart. Place it in a small jar with any leftover herb powder and seal it tight.

Light the black candle and say:

"Your words fall silent, your deeds unmade.
By root and blade, your noise shall fade.
I call for peace, not harm or fight—
But you'll speak no more if you speak not right."

Seal the jar with wax and store it out of sight.
Dispose of the jar when the situation is resolved.

SPELL TO CLEANSE A SPACE OF OLD ENERGY

Cards: Four of Swords, The World, Ace of Wands
Tools: White candle, sage or rosemary bundle, sea salt, glass bowl, broom, bell, open window

The Four of Swords goes at the heart of the working—this is the call to rest and quiet. The World is placed to the east for closure and completeness. The Ace of Wands is laid to the west to invoke new energy and vitality.

Start by sweeping the space clockwise, physically or symbolically, to stir stagnant energy. Place the cards near the center of the room and light the white candle. Burn rosemary or sage, fanning smoke into corners while ringing the bell once per room.

Fill the glass bowl with water and a generous pinch of sea salt. Stir it clockwise and say:

"What's stale be stirred, what's wrong be right,
I cleanse this place by flame and light.
By sword and world and wand anew,
This space is whole, clear, strong, and true."

Leave the candle burning until the air feels lighter or let it burn all the way down. Pour the salt water at the base of a tree or down a natural drain. Store the Ace of Wands on your altar to maintain freshness in the space.

SPELL TO ATTRACT LOYAL FRIENDSHIPS

Cards: Three of Cups, Two of Wands, Knight of Pentacles
Tools: Pink or orange candle, honey, cinnamon stick, bay leaf, small dish, a lock of your hair or signature

Lay out the cards in a triangle: Three of Cups at the top for joyful connection, Two of Wands on the left to invite new beginnings, and the Knight of Pentacles on the right to anchor lasting loyalty.

Place a bay leaf, cinnamon stick, and a small spoonful of honey in a dish. Add a strand of your hair or a paper with your full name signed three times. Light the candle and hold your hands over the dish, saying:

"I call in friends both bold and kind,
Whose hearts are whole, whose words align.
Through joy and trust and steady ground,
Let kindred spirits now be found."

Let the candle burn for 15 minutes, then extinguish. Store the Three of Cups with the bay leaf in a safe space. If a new friendship begins in the next two weeks, stir a drop of the spell's honey into a shared drink to bless the bond.

SPELL FOR ENERGETIC REBIRTH
AFTER TRAUMA

Cards: Death, Judgement, The Fool
Tools: Black and white candles, salt, small bowl of milk or honey water, egg shell, written affirmation of rebirth

Lay Death on the left for release, Judgement in the center for spiritual renewal, and The Fool on the right for new beginnings. Create a line of salt beneath the cards to divide the past from the future.

Light the black candle and read your affirmation aloud:

"I am not what broke me. I am what rises."

Sit with Death and Judgement for a few minutes, letting go of what you've been holding. Then blow out the black candle and light the white one. Break the eggshell and crush it into the bowl of milk or honey water. Stir clockwise and say:

"What was lost has made me whole.
What I was has paid the toll.
I rise in truth, I rise in light—
My name is claimed, my will is right."

Drink or anoint yourself lightly with the milk mixture. Leave the Fool card on your altar for one full lunar cycle to walk with your new self.

SPELL TO ATTRACT AN ALIGNED ROMANTIC PARTNER

Cards: The Lovers, The Star, Queen of Cups
Tools: Pink candle, rose quartz, apple slices, honey, red thread, glass jar, small photo or symbolic token

Place The Lovers at the base of your working as the intention. The Star goes above it to guide with clarity, and the Queen of Cups to the side to attract loving, emotionally available energy. Write your desires—not physical traits, but emotional qualities—on a piece of paper. Be specific.

Place the note in the jar with three apple slices and a spoonful of honey. Add the rose quartz and a symbolic token (a heart charm, a ribbon, or a pressed flower). Tie the jar shut with red thread and seal it with pink candle wax. Say:

*"I call for love that honors me.
A bond that's open, kind, and free.
By heart and star and sacred cup,
Let love that's true come rising up."*

Keep the jar on your altar for 21 days. Speak your desires aloud to it each night. If love appears and feels aligned, bury the jar under a rose bush or flowering plant to bless the relationship.

SPELL TO SHIFT A NEGATIVE
REPUTATION OR UNJUST JUDGMENT

Cards: The Hanged Man, Justice, Six of Wands
Tools: White candle, sunflower petals, sugar, parchment, mirror, clear quartz

Lay The Hanged Man in the center to represent suspended perception or misunderstanding. Place Justice to the left, calling for correction and truth. Set Six of Wands to the right, invoking recognition and restored respect. On parchment, write your name and a statement of how you wish to be perceived—truthfully and powerfully. Fold it toward you three times.

Place the folded paper beneath the mirror. Sprinkle sunflower petals and sugar over the mirror to sweeten your image and reflect back clarity. Light the white candle beside the layout. Hold the quartz in your hand and say:

"Let what is false fall away,
And let what's true be seen today.
Not by rumor, not by tale,
But by the truth that will prevail."

Keep the mirror and paper together on your altar for six days. On the seventh, burn the parchment and bury the ashes near your front door. Place the Six of Wands under your pillow for ongoing support.

SPELL FOR PSYCHIC PROTECTION
WHILE READING FOR OTHERS

Cards: The High Priestess, Seven of Wands, Queen of Swords
Tools: Purple candle, obsidian, rosemary, protective oil, white cloth, your deck

Lay The High Priestess as the guide and gatekeeper. Below her, place Seven of Wands for defensive spiritual posture. Lay the Queen of Swords to the side as your boundary-setting voice. Dress the purple candle with protective oil and burn rosemary as incense.

Place your tarot deck on a white cloth between the cards. Set the obsidian on top of the deck. Light the candle and say:

"I read with clarity, not fear.
No shade may cross my circle here.
Let voice be true, let eyes be sharp—
And none may reach who bear ill heart."

Keep the deck in the white cloth when not in use. Repeat this spell monthly or after any reading that leaves you feeling drained. You may also anoint the Queen of Swords card and place it beneath the deck before client readings.

SPELL TO BREAK FREE FROM A REPEATING MISTAKE OR PATTERN

Cards: The Wheel of Fortune, The Tower, Ace of Swords

Tools: Black candle, lemon peel, iron key, written description of the pattern, scissors, bowl of water

Lay The Wheel of Fortune at the top to represent cycles. Below it, place The Tower to break the pattern and the Ace of Swords beneath that for clean release. Write a full description of the repeated pattern or mistake on paper. Be honest, specific, and complete. Fold the paper once and place it under The Tower.

Anoint the candle with lemon oil or rub it with fresh peel. Place the key over the Ace of Swords. Light the candle and say:

"This pattern ends, I see it now.
No more the same, I shift somehow.
By word and will and breaking flame,
I cut this loop, I change the game."

Cut the written paper into pieces with scissors. Drop them into a bowl of water and extinguish the candle. Pour the water down the drain or at a crossroads. Keep the key with you as a reminder that you hold the door to change. Some say that putting out a candle cancels out the spell. I was always taught that if the act of putting it out is part of the spell and planned that way – it is just fine to do so.

SPELL TO EMPOWER PUBLIC SPEAKING OR STAGE PERFORMANCE

Cards: The Sun, King of Wands, Knight of Swords
Tools: Orange candle, throat-soothing tea (like licorice or peppermint), tiger's eye, gold pen, speech notes or performance item

Place The Sun at the top of the spread for radiance and charisma. King of Wands to the left for presence and control. Knight of Swords to the right for clarity, speed, and effective delivery. Drink a warm cup of tea to open and soothe the voice.

Place your written speech, outline, or object (such as a microphone or performance script) beneath the three cards. Light the candle and hold the tiger's eye in your palm while saying:

"Let my voice strike sure and bright.
Let nerves be calm and words take flight.
By wand and sword and sun above,
I speak with fire, with grace, with love."

Anoint your throat and lips with a drop of herbal tea or just the throat if you have a skin-safe essential oil blend. Dilute with a carrier oil if needed. Carry the tiger's eye into your presentation or performance space. Store The Sun card with your materials until the event has passed.

SPELL TO ATTRACT CLIENTS OR CUSTOMERS TO A SPIRITUAL OR MAGICAL BUSINESS

Cards: The Magician, Three of Pentacles, Queen of Wands
Tools: Green or gold candle, business card or offering flyer, cinnamon, basil, small magnet, written statement of service

Lay The Magician in the center to represent your business power. Three of Pentacles on the left for collaboration and shared skill. Queen of Wands on the right to draw attention and inspire trust. Place your business card or flyer beneath the layout with a statement like: "I offer valuable service to those who seek it."

Sprinkle cinnamon and basil over the cards. Set the magnet on top of the business card. Light the candle and say:

*"Let those who seek, now seek me.
Let what I give be seen clearly.
By flame and craft and pentacle's might,
Let need and gift align in light."*

Let the candle burn while visualizing people finding you with ease. Carry the magnet or business card to any in-person events. Repeat under waxing moons or on Thursdays for financial and social expansion.

CONCLUSION

Tarot magic isn't something you finish—it's something you grow with. The more you show up to the cards, the more they show up for you. Whether you're casting, divining, or healing after a ritual, the deck remains your mirror and your ally.

By now, you know how to structure a spell, read the suits, speak to spirits, and work with intention. You've moved from guessing to choosing. From reaction to direction.

The key thing to remember is this: your will leads the work. Tarot responds to clarity and purpose. Half-hearted effort brings half-hearted results. But when you cast with focus and faith, the deck rises to meet you.

You don't need to know everything. Just stay curious. Reflect, adapt, and keep working. Let the cards become a living part of your path. And trust that your magic will always lead you in the right direction.

TAROT QUICK REFERENCE GUIDE

This guide is designed for fast reference during spellwork, readings, and altar setups. Use it to recall keywords, elemental energies, magical uses, and symbolic purposes. Add your own notes in the margins or blank pages to personalize it further as your relationship with the cards evolves.

MAJOR ARCANA

The Fool (0)
Element: Air
Keywords: New beginnings, freedom, trust, leap of faith
Magical Uses: Starting new journeys, clearing fear, releasing attachments, calling in possibility

The Magician (1)
Element: Air
Keywords: Manifestation, willpower, tools, personal power
Magical Uses: Skill-building, focused spellwork, confidence, activating personal magic

The High Priestess (2)
Element: Water
Keywords: Intuition, mystery, hidden knowledge, inner voice
Magical Uses: Spirit communication, dreamwork,

moon rituals, uncovering truth

The Empress (3)
Element: Earth
Keywords: Abundance, creation, nurturing, fertility
Magical Uses: Prosperity, love and beauty magic, growth spells, sacred femininity

The Emperor (4)
Element: Fire
Keywords: Authority, stability, structure, discipline
Magical Uses: Protection, leadership work, financial stability, healthy boundaries

The Hierophant (5)
Element: Earth
Keywords: Tradition, spiritual lineage, teachings, values
Magical Uses: Ancestral magic, spiritual education, rituals of initiation and oath

The Lovers (6)
Element: Air
Keywords: Union, choices, harmony, relationship
Magical Uses: Love spells, commitment work, union of opposites, heart healing

The Chariot (7)
Element: Water
Keywords: Momentum, control, success through effort
Magical Uses: Goal-setting, motivation, cutting

through resistance, energy direction

Strength (8)
Element: Fire
Keywords: Courage, endurance, calm power, inner control
Magical Uses: Emotional regulation, resilience, overcoming fear, empowerment spells

The Hermit (9)
Element: Earth
Keywords: Solitude, wisdom, introspection, guidance
Magical Uses: Self-inquiry, retreat rituals, seeking divine insight, soul work

Wheel of Fortune (10)
Element: Fire
Keywords: Change, cycles, fate, turning points
Magical Uses: Luck work, transformation spells, breaking cycles, timing clarity

Justice (11)
Element: Air
Keywords: Truth, fairness, accountability, karmic law
Magical Uses: Legal matters, balance spells, restoring order, spiritual contracts

The Hanged Man (12)
Element: Water
Keywords: Release, perspective, suspension,

sacrifice

Magical Uses: Letting go, ego dissolution, surrender rituals, spiritual pause

Death (13)

Element: Water

Keywords: Endings, transformation, renewal, closure

Magical Uses: Cord cutting, ancestor rites, major life transitions, rebirth

Temperance (14)

Element: Fire

Keywords: Harmony, balance, moderation, healing

Magical Uses: Energetic alignment, integration spells, balancing extremes

The Devil (15)

Element: Earth

Keywords: Temptation, control, shadow, unhealthy bonds

Magical Uses: Banishing, hexbreaking, shadow integration, addiction release

The Tower (16)

Element: Fire

Keywords: Disruption, truth revealed, sudden change, collapse

Magical Uses: Breaking illusions, destruction of old patterns, spiritual cleansing

The Star (17)

Element: Air
Keywords: Hope, healing, spiritual guidance,
blessings
Magical Uses: Cleansing, inspiration, altar devotion,
energetic recovery

The Moon (18)
Element: Water
Keywords: Dreams, illusion, psychic awareness, fear
Magical Uses: Shadow work, intuition, trance
journeys, uncovering secrets

The Sun (19)
Element: Fire
Keywords: Success, joy, clarity, radiance
Magical Uses: Abundance spells, solar rituals,
happiness, empowerment

Judgement (20)
Element: Fire
Keywords: Awakening, rebirth, resolution, higher
calling
Magical Uses: Past life healing, spiritual renewal,
calling in your true path

The World (21)
Element: Earth
Keywords: Completion, wholeness, integration,
fulfillment
Magical Uses: Closure, manifestation work,
finishing cycles, celebration

SUIT OF WANDS – FIRE ELEMENT

The Wands are aligned with fire and represent action, willpower, ambition, and movement. Use Wands cards when casting for drive, motivation, confidence, and breaking inertia.

Ace of Wands – The spark, inspiration, a new project beginning

Two of Wands – Decision-making, exploring options, strategic planning

Three of Wands – Growth, return on effort, long-term vision

Four of Wands – Stability, home blessings, sacred gatherings

Five of Wands – Conflict, competition, asserting your space

Six of Wands – Victory, success, recognition, standing out

Seven of Wands – Defense, standing firm, magical resilience

Eight of Wands – Fast movement, alignment, messages and travel

Nine of Wands – Boundaries, grit, enduring through difficulty

Ten of Wands – Burden, overload, taking on too much—time to release

Page of Wands – Excitement, youthful fire, new magical exploration

Knight of Wands – Boldness, ambition, risk-taking, passionate drive

Queen of Wands – Charisma, self-assurance, natural leadership, solar magic

King of Wands – Visionary leadership, entrepreneurial fire, bold strategy

SUIT OF CUPS – WATER ELEMENT

Cups govern your emotions, intuition, healing energy, relationships, and the unseen. Use Cups cards in love spells, grief work, sadness, dreamwork, and ancestor veneration.

Ace of Cups – Open heart, new emotional beginning, sacred self-love

Two of Cups – Partnership, romantic union, harmony

Three of Cups – Celebration, friendship, emotional support

Four of Cups – Emotional stagnation, apathy, needing perspective

Five of Cups – Loss, grief, sorrow, what's been left behind

Six of Cups – Nostalgia, memory, childhood healing, sweetness

Seven of Cups – Illusions, confusion, too many choices

Eight of Cups – Walking away, emotional boundaries, closure

Nine of Cups – Wish fulfilled, satisfaction, magical completion

Ten of Cups – Emotional abundance, spiritual

family, fulfillment

Page of Cups – Intuition awakening, creative beginnings, gentle energy

Knight of Cups – Romance, charm, pursuit of beauty and love

Queen of Cups – Psychic power, empathy, compassion, dream magic

King of Cups – Emotional maturity, diplomacy, healer archetype

SUIT OF SWORDS – AIR ELEMENT

Swords represent thought, truth, logic, decisions, and the realm of the mind. Use Swords in protection, banishment, justice, and clarity spells.

Ace of Swords – Breakthrough, truth revealed, mental clarity

Two of Swords – Stalemate, choices avoided, intuitive impasse

Three of Swords – Heartbreak, betrayal, painful truth

Four of Swords – Rest, recovery, spiritual retreat

Five of Swords – Conflict, strategy, winning at a cost

Six of Swords – Transition, moving forward, energetic migration

Seven of Swords – Deception, trickery, stealth and protection

Eight of Swords – Feeling trapped, mental restriction, limiting beliefs

Nine of Swords – Anxiety, overthinking, emotional torment

Ten of Swords – Finality, betrayal, painful but necessary ending

Page of Swords – Curiosity, new ideas, sharp mind awakening

Knight of Swords – Quick action, fierce focus, determination

Queen of Swords – Wisdom, discernment, truth without emotion

King of Swords – Authority, justice, clear communication

SUIT OF PENTACLES – EARTH ELEMENT

Pentacles govern the material world: money, work, health, home, and physical safety. Use Pentacles in prosperity spells, grounding, stability work, and body-focused magic.

Ace of Pentacles – New opportunity, seed of wealth, manifestation begins

Two of Pentacles – Balance, time management, juggling priorities

Three of Pentacles – Teamwork, shared goals, collaboration

Four of Pentacles – Saving, protecting resources, holding too tightly

Five of Pentacles – Lack, hardship, support needed, poverty mindset

Six of Pentacles – Generosity, financial flow,

energy exchange

Seven of Pentacles – Long-term vision, investment, patience

Eight of Pentacles – Mastery, focus, refining skills

Nine of Pentacles – Independence, luxury, hard-earned rewards

Ten of Pentacles – Legacy, generational wealth, long-term success

Page of Pentacles – New studies, job offers, stable beginnings

Knight of Pentacles – Responsibility, diligence, slow and steady growth

Queen of Pentacles – Nurturer, abundance, earth-magic matriarch

King of Pentacles – Provider, business success, grounded power

BIBLIOGRAPHY

Greer, Mary K. *Tarot for Your Self: A Workbook for Personal Transformation.* New Page Books. 2002.

Pollack, Rachel. *Seventy-Eight Degrees of Wisdom: A Book of Tarot.* Weiser Books. 1980.

Place, Robert M. *The Tarot: History, Symbolism, and Divination.* TarcherPerigee. 2005.

Cunningham, Scott. *Divination for Beginners: Reading the Past, Present & Future.* Llewellyn Publications. 1989.

Dugan, Ellen. *Tarot Witchery: Using the Cards for Spellwork, Ritual, and Magick.* Llewellyn Publications. 2024.

Matthews, Caitlín. *The Celtic Book of the Dead: A Guide for Your Voyage to the Celtic Otherworld.* Destiny Books. 1992.

D'Este, Sorita & Rankine, David. *Practical Elemental Magick: Working the Magick of the Four Elements in the Western Mystery Tradition.* Avalonia. 2008.

Illes, Judika. *Encyclopedia of 5,000 Spells – The Ultimate Reference Book for the Magical Arts.* Harper Collins. 2008.

Wright, Elbee. *Book of Legendary Spells.* Marlar Publishing Co. 1968.

Yronwode, Catherine & White, Gregory Lee. *Amulets, Charms, and Talismans in the Hoodoo and Conjure Tradition.* Lucky Mojo Curio Company Publishing. 2021.

Hyatt, Harry Middleton. *Hoodoo, Conjuration, Witchcraft, and Rootwork, Volumes 1 - 5.* Memoirs of the Alma C. Hyatt Foundation. 1970–1978.

Bacon, Alice. "Conjuring and Conjure-Doctors." *Southern Workman* Issue 28, 1895.

Oliver, Mark. "Unleashing the Power of the Gods: Hexes and Black Magic in the Ancient Greek Olympics." *Ancient Origins* July, 2017.

Giralt, Sebastia. "Medieval Necromancy – The Art of Controlling Demons." *Sciencia.cat.*

Downton, Dawn Rae. *The Little Book of Curses and Maledictions for Everyday Use.* Skyhorse Publishing. 2009.

White, Gregory Lee. *The Use of Magical Oils in Hoodoo, Prayer, and Spellwork.* White Willow Press. 2017.

Johnson Smith & Co. *The Book of Forbidden Knowledge: Black Magic, Superstition, Charms, and Divination.* Circa 1920.

www.ingramcontent.com/pod-product-compliance
Lightning Source LLC
Chambersburg PA
CBHW061806120626
46550CB00005B/2162